T0156496

HOW TO CONTROL YOUR CAREER FOR LIFE

HELPFUL TECHNIQUES FOR GETTING, KEEPING, AND CHANGING EMPLOYMENT OPPORTUNITIES

DONALD FORD

IUNIVERSE, INC.
NEW YORK   BLOOMINGTON

How to Control Your Career for Life
Helpful Techniques for Getting, Keeping, and
Changing Employment Opportunities

Copyright © 2009 by Donald Ford

All rights reserved. No part of this book may be used or reproduced by any means,
graphic, electronic, or mechanical, including photocopying, recording, taping or by any
information storage retrieval system without the written permission of the publisher
except in the case of brief quotations embodied in critical articles and reviews.

The views expressed in this work are solely those of the author and do not necessarily reflect the views
of the publisher, and the publisher hereby disclaims any responsibility for them.

iUniverse books may be ordered through booksellers or by contacting:

iUniverse
1663 Liberty Drive
Bloomington, IN 47403
www.iuniverse.com
1-800-Authors (1-800-288-4677)

Because of the dynamic nature of the Internet, any Web addresses or links contained in this book
may have changed since publication and may no longer be valid.

ISBN: 978-1-4401-8272-3 (sc)
ISBN: 978-1-4401-8274-7 (dj)
ISBN: 978-1-4401-8273-0 (ebk)

Printed in the United States of America

iUniverse rev. date: 12/29/2009

DEDICATION

I would like to thank my wife, Frances, for her constant help and encouragement and my late dad, Wilfrid Ford, who was in the publishing business all his life, first at the Oxford Press, then at McClelland and Stewart, and finally as founding president of Doubleday Canada.

CONTENTS

PREFACE

You may be employed in a company that is in transition, you may be ready to enter the job market, or your company may look quite secure. Whatever the situation, you will find this book helpful.

You may have heard the company president say, "As long as I am president, you will have a job here," and three weeks later, you are laid off and are looking for a new job. You will say this is not fair, and it probably isn't, but it is the reality you have to live with.

Many companies are in transition because of a number of factors. These could include a changing economic climate, new senior management, downsizing, plant closure, mergers, bankruptcy, or production moving to another country. These changes can be like an economic earthquake, and it is vital that you learn how to control your career. No one can do this for you; it is something you must learn to do for yourself.

We regularly read unemployment statistics both in the United States and Canada. For example, here is a quote from the November 2008 statistics from the U.S. Department of Labor's Web site:[1]

> Non-farm employment fell sharply (-533,000) in November, and the unemployment rate rose from 6.6 to 6.7 percent. November's drop in payroll employment declined followed by declines of 403,000 in September and 320,000 in October, as revised. Job losses were large and widespread across the major industry sectors in November.

The rate as of January 9, 2009, is 7.2 percent.

1   www.bls.gov

The statistics from Canada are about the same. Here is a quote from the November report, dated December 5, 2008, from Statistics Canada:[2]

> Following little change in October, employment fell by 71,000 in November, with the decrease split between full and part time work. The unemployment rate rose 0.1 percentage points to 6.3%.

It is now 6.65 as of January 9, 2009.

In contrast to these numbers, the unemployment rate during the Great Depression of the 1930s was 25 percent. These numbers, along with news about huge corporations like General Motors and Lehman Brothers, can be very depressing.

However, the fact is that some companies are still hiring people. For example, Research in Motion, which produces the famous Blackberry, is looking for 902 employees in North and South America; 139 in Europe, the Middle East, and Africa; and 94 in the Asia-Pacific area.

General Electric has 1,669 positions in the United States as posted on its Web site.

I want to emphasize that there are jobs out there, although you may have to work harder to find them.

In addition, you might also want to consider self-employment. I talk about that later in this book.

This book was written to help you control your career cycle of getting a job, keeping a job, and changing jobs. More people will be caught in layoffs in the near future than in the last ten years. The numbers above demonstrate the reality. I have been laid off twice and know the empty feeling you have when Monday morning comes and you don't go to work.

You may be asking about my qualifications for writing a book about controlling your career. Here is my story.

Several years ago, I was asked by a major multinational company to establish a career development system for a large group of their employees. I knew quite a bit about careers from my own experience but not in a systematic way. So I did what I always do when facing a

---

2   www.statcan.gc.ca

new challenge: I did a lot of reading and research until I knew what I was doing. I have listed the books I consulted in the bibliography.

I have had a variety of jobs. They include dishwasher, third cook, retail salesperson, recreational camp director, technical English instructor, seminar leader, and college administrator. Let me expand on my college work. I started two major departments: continuing education and the school of tourism. In the school of tourism, we designed and taught entry-level courses such as cooking, housekeeping, front-office reception, and marketing.

In addition, I served as chair on the following committees and boards: a committee of TV Ontario, the education committee of the board of the Tourism Industry Association of Canada, and the personnel committee of the board of the Inter-Varsity Christian Fellowship of Canada. These positions introduced me to a variety of industries and men and women at senior levels.

I have a BA from the University of Toronto and an MEd from the University of Calgary where I concentrated on college administration and adult education.

I have given you a bit of my background to show you that I have had exposure to a wide variety of occupations.

This book is based on what I learned from my own experience and the experiences of others.

Some people think that careers only apply to professionals or managers, but actually, everyone has a career. A career is simply a way of making a living.

For example, after graduating from high school, a friend of mine, Bruce Long, started to work in the housing industry. He did that for five years, and during that time, he completed his apprenticeship and earned his certificate of qualification as a carpenter. He and a friend decided to start their own house-building company and have a small group of employees. They have learned all the new techniques of building energy-efficient houses. They concentrate on upper-middle-class homes and build five or six homes in the $500,000 range each year. They have done very well and have orders for all of 2009.

After you have been laid off, the first step is getting a new job. The second is keeping it, and then comes the time to change jobs. That is what this book is all about. So how do we go about doing these things?

You need to work at getting a job you like and one that you are good at for two reasons. First, you will spend a lot of time working, so do not—if you possibly can avoid it—spend your time doing something you do not like or even hate.

Second, you need to earn all you can. As John Wesley said, "Earn all you can, keep what you need, and give the rest away." In this way, you can provide for yourself and your family and contribute to making the world a better place.

When I was quite a bit younger, one of my mentors, Charles Phillips, emphasized the importance of having an overall purpose in life. Now we talk about having a mission or central purpose in life. When I was in my twenties, I remember very vividly my mentor saying, "Ford, what are you going to do with your life?" That question made me realize that my life counted for something. At age thirty, we only have around 420 months left in our working lives, so get busy and do something.

The advice in this book, if acted upon, will save you a lot of headaches, time, and money. I have put a lot of ideas together which will be very helpful but only if you put them into practice.

I want to acknowledge Richard Bowles, who wrote *What Color Is Your Parachute*. I attended his four-day seminar several years ago, and he had a profound influence on me. His thinking is reflected in this book.

I wish you every success, and God bless you in this very important activity.

Chapter One

Basic Foundations for Controlling Your Career

A career is made up of a number of jobs. It is like walking along a path, and on the way, you do a number of things especially related to work. The word comes from the Roman world where they used the Latin word *carraria* for a road on which they drove their chariots.

I will use the word *career* to refer to the whole process of getting, keeping, and changing jobs.

While writing this book, I was often reminded of people or incidents that illustrated the point I was making. I always refer to real people, but I use different names.

A career can be any occupation, from a dishwasher to a company president or from a volunteer to a highly paid basketball player; it does not just refer to upper-level jobs.

A career is made up of a number of jobs. You will probably change jobs ten or more times in your working career, so it is important that you learn how to get a job quickly and with as little stress as possible. This change can occur within the company you work in or you may move to another company.

To get and keep a job, you must meet the needs of the organization.

If you are self-employed, you must meet your customers' needs for your goods or services.

This book will outline a process you can use all your working life. Working can give you a lot of satisfaction, provide financially for you and your family, enable you to make a contribution to your organization, and give you the means to make the world a better place. This book will also help you take the initiative in either developing your career in an organization or in finding a new job.

Here are five key questions this book will help you answer:

- What are my skills?
- Where can I use them?
- How can I get a job?
- How can I make a contribution in my present and future jobs?
- How do I handle changing jobs?

WHY IS PLANNING A CAREER SO IMPORTANT?

In the present economic climate, controlling your career is not an option; it is an absolute necessity. Here are four reasons.

First, you will spend a lot of time working. Say you start working when you are twenty years old and work until you are sixty-five. The time spent working will be 2,250 weeks or 90,000 hours. Wow! If at all possible, be sure you spend most of your time doing something you like to do and do well.

Second, you will earn a lot of money. Assume you earn $20,000 the first year and $75,000 the last year of work and you work thirty-five years.

Use this formula to determine your lifetime income:

$$\text{Years of work} \times \frac{\text{starting salary} + \text{final salary}}{2} = \text{total income}$$

$$35 \times \frac{\$20,000 + \$75,000}{2} = \$1,332,500$$

Work this out for yourself.

$$\text{Years of work} \times \frac{\text{your present salary} + \text{final salary}}{2} = \text{total income}$$

Even at minimum wage of $7.00 an hour, you will earn $630,000.

You are in charge of a project with an income of well over a million dollars. So plan it carefully and well.

Third, as I said before, you will likely change jobs about ten times or even more during your working career. At the present time, many companies are laying off workers, and they will all be changing jobs, although some may be called back. It is very difficult to predict the future; all you can do is focus on the present and plan for the future. Here is a list of recent layoffs in the United States.

Omnicom	3,000
Western Digital	2,500
Cooper Tire	1,400
Aetna Insurance	1,000
Bristol-Myers Squibb	800
Sirius Radio	458
Las Vegas Sands Hotel	200

In Canada, the numbers are lower because it is a smaller country; here are some numbers.

Bell Canada	2,500
Bombardier Recreation	1,370
Daimier Trucks	1,300
Air Canada	500
North American Palladium	350
Global TV	200

These are in addition to the layoffs in the automobile sector and parts manufacturing.

At the time of this writing, I had just read about Alcoa laying off 13,500 workers in Canada and the United States and Rio Tinto laying off 14,000 workers worldwide. Employment was more or less stable when I first started writing this book; it is a far different situation now.

This book has real-life examples of people who have just entered the workforce or who have been laid off and gotten new jobs.

This book will help you through this very difficult time. It will help you get a job quickly and with as little stress as possible.

Finally, through working, you can make the world a better place, socially and economically. For example, for a number of years, I taught technical English at a technical college. While there, I showed students how to write technical reports and résumés, how to make technical presentations, and how to develop a lot of other useful skills. Later, I helped start new divisions in a new college, which enabled young men and women to earn a good living. In this way, I helped to provide for my family and made my little world a better place economically and socially. You can do the same.

THE IDEAL JOB

In searching for the ideal job for you, you need to take into consideration three things: your skills and abilities, your goals in life, and the job market. The place where they overlap gives you an idea of your ideal job.

Let me begin with a ridiculous example.

In the area of skills, Harry is persuasive and likes working with computers but hates exercising. He is a bit of a slob and avoids the gym at all costs. Harry's goal in life is to earn a lot of money, so he looks at the job market and realizes that professional wrestlers receive high salaries. Harry steps into the ring; he lasts maybe ten seconds before being thrown into the audience.

Here are better examples.

George is an excellent carpenter and cabinetmaker, has good sales ability, and decides to make horse-drawn buggies like he has seen in Western movies. He also wants to earn a decent income to provide for his family. George is in a better position than Harry, but the demand for horse-drawn buggies is limited and he would need to work hard to find a market. His ability to provide for his family could be limited.

The other night, I watched a TV show about an attractive young woman who loved making her own clothes but decided she wanted to be a model in New York City. They told her that in order to succeed, she needed to have some plastic surgery done on her face. During one of the interviews, she wore some exotic, colorful clothes that she had made. One of the executives was so impressed with her outfit that she asked her to work in their design department. As a result, she dropped the modeling career and went into the clothing-design business. I thought this was a useful example of this young woman using the skills she had rather than the ones she did not have.

Here is another good example.

Mary has above-average intelligence. She is very good at explaining ideas, is quite self-assured but not pushy, is able to study and pass examinations, and is persistent. She started her working life as a teacher and was very successful. Later, she wanted to learn about the real estate business because she and her husband were thinking about selling their house. She also liked the idea of earning an above-average salary. She learned about the real estate market and decided to start. The first year, her earnings were quite low; however, she persisted and after two years became one of the top producers in her company. She went on and earned her broker's license. She used her skills and special knowledge. Also note that she changed her career after learning about the new business.

A word of caution—and I will say more about this later—every job has parts of it that you are not good at or you do not like. But these things have to be done and are part of the job. These aspects might be a third of the job or more. These weaknesses can be minefields or, to use a boating term, shoals. If you do not overcome these things and learn to deal with them, they will wreck your career and you will not achieve your potential. So when you look at a job, realize that there are things in the job you must overcome or you will not survive.

So it is important that you know what you can do and do well, know what is important in life, can meet a need in the job market, and know and overcome your weaknesses.

On the next page, you have room to expand on your career goals.

WHAT CAN YOU EXPECT TO GET OUT OF THIS BOOK?

Please take a few minutes now to write out how you expect to profit from working your way through this book.

Here is how I hope you profit from this book: First, you find or maintain a job that you like doing, that you do well, and that meets your goals in life. Second, you know your weaknesses and are able to overcome them. Third, you are able to change jobs with as little stress as possible.

GET SOMEONE YOU TRUST TO HELP YOU

Find a mentor who is able to help you through this process. Remember, this is a million-dollar project you are working on, and it is one of the most important activities in your entire life. It will affect your health, family, wealth, and place in society. You need all the help you can get.

A mentor is a wise and trusted guide. I talk about first, finding a mentor; second, what qualities to look for; third, what to do in a mentoring relationship; and finally, developing the relationship.

The first question is "How do I find a mentor?" If you are a recent graduate from a training school, apprenticeship program, college, or university, ask if the institution offers a mentoring service. Many will be able to help you.

If you are on your own, try to find someone you respect and admire. He or she may be a friend or acquaintance, a member of your professional association, or someone in your field of work. Sometimes, it is a good idea to choose someone outside of your field because they may be more objective and see things that an insider would not see. Basically, look for someone you feel comfortable with. Do not choose your supervisor at work; their function is quite different from that of a mentor. I would also be cautious about choosing someone at your place of work.

The second question is "What qualities should I look for?" The person should be someone, as I said above, whom you admire and respect from your field of work. My advice is that men should mentor men and women mentor women.

Your mentor should have the following characteristics. He or she should be:

- Someone with whom you can be open and share your successes and failures and who will not judge you
- A good listener
- Comfortable in giving feedback—positive or negative—challenging you to keep moving forward
- Positive, upbeat
- Available, reliable, and interested
- Someone who knows your current employment situation
- Creative and someone who will ask if you have considered …?
- Trustworthy and someone who can keep a confidence

You should avoid:

- A person who is too controlling
- A person who makes you feel uncomfortable
- A person who seems to know all the answers

7

The third question is "What do you do in a mentoring relationship?" The first meeting should be an informal one. Explain your situation, that you are about to enter the job market or are employed or have been recently laid off and are looking for work. See if the person is interested in helping you and also whether this person meets some or all of the above qualifications. This could all be done informally. If you want to keep going, try to set up another time to meet. Pay for the lunch if you meet at a restaurant.

This book is a workbook, and you should share all your work with your mentor. In this way, you become accountable to him or her. For example, there is a section on goal setting and implementation. Your mentor can keep you on track with your implementation. You need to be accountable to your mentor to keep you going, especially if you have been laid off. Most people function better if they are accountable to someone.

As you progress through this book, I will make suggestions about things you could talk about with your mentor.

The final question is "How can you develop this process?" Make sure you both know the expectations. For example, I had a great mentor who had a very responsible position. He explained in a very nice way that the only time he thought about my work was when we talked. But when we met, he really listened and entered into the relationship. Decide how often you want to meet (e.g., monthly or when appropriate). Do not ask for too much. After all, your mentor is probably a busy person. Be sure to say, "Thank you," often, and when you get your new job or position, be sure to invite your mentor to your celebration.

Please make a list of two or three people who can mentor you in this very important work.

Potential Mentors	
1. _____	Date contacted __/___/____
2. _____	Date contacted __/___/____
3. _____	Date contacted __/___/____

Now that you have started with contacting your potential mentor, you can move on to the first step in controlling your career, which is discovering your skills.

This is not a "never-fail" method. The jobs may not be there just yet, or other more qualified applicants may get the job, and so on. This is a process which will require patience and persistence, so don't give up; keep learning, growing, and applying for the ideal job.

YOU ARE UNIQUE AND EXTRAORDINARY

A submarine is a very amazing, unique, and special kind of vessel. It can move around underwater for long periods of time and at high speeds. However, it would be silly to put a submarine on the runway at an airport with hopes that it would fly; no amount of persuasion would make it fly. After all, submarines have little wings and a propeller. Some people are like a submarine at an airport; they want to do something for which they are totally unfit.

There is only one person in the world like you. Look around and see for yourself. You are different from anyone else and were designed with a unique set of skills, talents, relationship skills, and physical characteristics. "Know yourself" and discover this most amazing person: you.

If you are about to enter the world of work, are underemployed, are working in a job you like but are uncertain about its viability, or have just been laid off, you are looking at an uncertain future. However, just remember that you are special and that you have a lot to offer.

√ Case Study: Dan

Here is a true story about a close friend who was laid off. Dan was very clever but before he could get established in a suitable job, he got married and started to have children. He took any job he could get and worked as a receiver in a plant. The company rule was that receivers were not allowed to go onto the delivery truck to help unload it. One night, a truck came and they asked him to come into the truck to help unload it. Unknown to him, he was being videotaped, and the next day, he was dismissed.

The city in which he lives has a large number of small manufacturing plants. He went door-to-door offering his services. By the end of the week, he had a much better job earning a lot more money as a printer. The interesting thing is that he did not have any experience as a printer, but during the interview, he so impressed the people that they hired him and trained him. He now operates a huge printing machine, the largest in the plant.

√ Case Study: Duncan

Here is another story, this time about a young man named Duncan. He had difficulty deciding what to do with his life; he knew that he wanted to help people and at college took outdoor education as his major in the education program. After graduation, he had difficulty finding a job in his field and started working part-time as an ambulance driver in a small town. This brought him into contact with the local hospital.

One day, one of the nurses told Duncan that she thought he would make a good nurse. Duncan had had academic difficulties while in high school and was not sure if he could handle the academic part of a nursing education. He enrolled in the biology course in the local high school and did very well. He had also done quite well at college. This boosted his confidence, and he enrolled in the nursing program at a community college. He found his niche and graduated as one of the top three students and is now working in a large hospital.

ACCEPT THE RESPONSIBILITY FOR USING YOUR ABILITIES

At the beginning of this book, I talked about this million-dollar project: your career. We are managers of this million-dollar project. The success of this project will largely depend on how well you use the abilities you have been given or you have developed. The tools are your skills and abilities. Many people with limited abilities, at least according to some people, go a long way because they work very hard with what they have.

As I mentioned earlier, I used to work at a technical college. I remember the head of the art department saying that the students who worked hard with their limited artistic ability went a lot further than the more talented ones because the more talented ones did not work as hard.

Here is an example. Roger came from a wealthy family. They sent him to a very exclusive private school where he did not do very well. One of his teachers said he would do much better if he did not spend so much time in the media club producing student television and radio shows.

After graduation, he joined the air force, and since he had an interest in radio and television, he was assigned to work in that area. After he left the air force, he went to university and after graduation did a variety of jobs. There was a motion picture production company in the city where he lived, and he got a job as a sound engineer. He finally got work in his field and used the skills that he had. During his career, he opened up four recording studios and worked with most of the major networks. I tell you this to encourage you to use the skills and abilities that you have.

So you are a manager or steward and are responsible for using the abilities you have. The more you use them, the more successful you will be.

You're already on your way to a better career! Here is what you've learned so far.

- Controlling your career is very important.

- The ideal job suits you and your needs—both economic and mental.
- This book will help you chart your course on this journey.
- Get someone to help you—a mentor is invaluable.
- You are unique and extraordinary.
- You can accept the responsibility for using your abilities.

In the next chapter, I show you how to discover your skills and abilities.

CHAPTER TWO

WHAT ARE YOUR SKILLS?

Let's begin the process of controlling your career by focusing on the key question: What are your skills and abilities? These are simply the things you do well and find satisfying. Realize you can do a lot of things. By the time you have finished this section, you will realize that you are more skilled and know more than you thought you did.

Some people have been told by others that they are dumb and stupid and can't do anything. Don't believe those lies; you have all sorts of abilities.

Here is an example. At age twenty-five, Ray Smith started his career by going door-to-door signing people up for a delivery service. He was very outgoing and did very well. His friends thought that was as far as he could go with his high-school education and limited skills. One day, he saw an advertisement in the paper for a job in the shopping center business. He applied, and to everyone's surprise, he got the job. He started working for one of the most successful businessmen in Canada. Very soon, he was developing shopping centers. He then moved to another part of the country and became vice president of a major real estate company. While there, he was involved in the community and was chairman of a very major community activity. Not bad for someone who, according to his friends, had limited abilities!

There are two kinds of skills; the first type includes what some people call transferable skills, and the second type includes technical skills or special knowledge. Knowing what these are is the key to doing a successful job.

TRANSFERABLE SKILLS

Transferable skills are ones that you use on every job. There are three types of transferable skills. The first type includes skills with people, like persuading or instructing. Salespeople and teachers use these types of skills. The second includes skills with data, like numbers. Accountants and actuaries use these skills. The third type involves skills with things like tools. Mechanics and surgeons use these types of skills.

These skills are like a tool kit a mechanic takes from job to job.

What skills does a teacher need? A baseball player? A truck driver? A brain surgeon? A third-world development worker? They all need different transferable skills.

Famous people are known for their skills. One example is Yousuf Karsh, portrait photographer. I met him when he was the judge at a photography show I entered when I was in university. He was a delightful man, and I was immediately drawn to him. This is a vital skill for a portrait photographer. He combined his ability to quickly relate to people with his technical skill to become a world-famous portrait photographer.

You need to know what you are good at and, further, what you enjoy doing—activities that give you satisfaction.

Let's take a look at how to identify your many skills.

HOW TO DISCOVER YOUR SKILLS AND DEVELOP A SKILLS INVENTORY

The identification of your skills is one of the keys to getting a job you can do well and will enjoy doing. When I say *enjoy*, I don't mean it will be easy. In most jobs, you will have to work hard, but you will find that you can do it and find pleasure in it.

In a previous example, I told about a real estate broker. She really liked helping people get a home they could afford and wanted to live in. In fact, if she felt that the buyer could not afford the house they wanted, she would say so. As a result, she lost some sales. At the same time, she worked long hours. Because of her dedication, she was one of the top realtors in her company.

I went through a process of finding out my skills similar to the process I am about to explain to you. At the end, I was able to write down on paper what I did well and what I enjoyed doing. I was quite delighted and surprised.

You will make your greatest contribution to your organization when you use your highest skills.

The best way that I know to identify your skills is to base your search on your past experiences.

For example, when one of our daughters was quite young, we gave her a real cooking set, one where you could actually make something, not just play at it. She loved cooking, and now, as an adult, she owns a very successful restaurant and is in the process of developing a second one.

First of all, look at the following chart called "My Accomplishments." You can see it is divided into sections of ten years. If you are in your twenties, make the divisions smaller. Think of two or three things you accomplished during each period of your life. This could be at work, at home, at school, or in a leisure activity. You took an action, solved a problem, or drew a picture, and it had concrete results. In addition, include experiences that you enjoyed and that you found satisfying not just pleasurable.

For example, when I was in grade five or six, we were told to draw a picture of anything we wanted. For some reason, we drew the pictures standing at the sides and back of the room. I drew a picture of water with some clouds and a few birds. I remember drawing the horizon toward the bottom of the page. To my surprise, the teacher liked my simple picture. I am interested in photography and still find that I am taking pictures of clouds. That's my accomplishment for my early years. I am sure you can do better than that.

Just briefly outline two or three accomplishments for each period of time. This whole activity might take a while, so don't rush it. Take a whole evening or longer if needed. This exercise is the foundation of your work. I have extra copies in the back of the book so you can make photocopies.

My Accomplishments

Ages
1–10_____

_____
_____
_____

11–20_____

_____
_____
_____

21–30_____

_____
_____

31–40_____

_____
_____

41–50_____

_____
_____
_____

Now pick one accomplishment from each section and write out as much detail as you can remember, with the emphasis on what you did. Leave a two-inch margin on the left or right side of the page. Try to get seven accomplishments to write about. If needed, use a separate piece of paper for each accomplishment.

I have given an example from my life at the end of this section incorporating all the main points. Here is a sample from that longer example.

I was the manager of a summer recreational children's camp which was situated on an island. We decided to purchase a larger boat. I talked to a friend who was responsible for a small hotel also situated on an island. We visited various boatbuilders to get more ideas and estimate costs. We decided to get a boat large enough to handle about thirty passengers and to handle all kinds of weather. We talked to the forestry company, which had a small fleet of boats that they used to pull log booms. They told us about a company that they used, and we decided to use the same company. They drew the plans, which we approved, and in the spring, we took delivery of the forty-eight-foot diesel-powered steel boat.

The skills I used were
- Decision making
- Consulting
- Comparing
- Researching
- Persuading

My Top Seven Accomplishments (A copy for photocopying is available in the back of the book.)

First Accomplishment	Skills

Second Accomplishment	Skills

Third Accomplishment	Skills

Fourth Accomplishment	Skills

Fifth Accomplishment	Skills

Sixth Accomplishment	Skills

Donald Ford

Seventh Accomplishment	Skills

Now take a look at your first accomplishment and underline as many skills as you can see and write them in the margin. These could be with people, data, or things.

There are two Web sites that you will find helpful in listing skills. They give lists of all the skills used in working. Take a look at them and list skills you may have missed. The first Web site is www.cdm. uwaterloo.ca. Click on "Self Assessment."

The second Web site to look at is www.occupationalinfo.org. Click on "Contents" and then "Appendix B." This gives a detailed list and explanation of skills which are divided into three groups: skills with data, skills with people, and skills with things.

This Web site is also useful in finding out what skills are needed for different jobs. Click on "ONET." Pick your occupation and look at all the details, especially skills needed. The "Crosswalk" leads to more detailed job descriptions.

After you have made your skill list, share your stories with your mentor to see if he or she can identify skills you missed. I did this during a workshop and was surprised to see the additional skills the group identified.

From this list, you will be able to see many of your skills. In fact, as you work through these stories, you will start to see a repetition of certain skills.

Make a list of these skills and put them in order of priority. Put your top skill at the top, followed by the next best, and so on. Try to get a job that matches your top skills.

Let me say a word about IQ tests. They are excellent; however, sometimes, they are not accurate. For example, I know of two people who scored very low but went on to get university degrees. In fact, one ended up as a university professor teaching psychology. He told his class that when he graduated from high school, he was advised not to go on to university. He went to university and did so well that he decided to go on to graduate school. Once again, he was told that he would have difficulty. On the way to graduate school, he was able to look at his student records and saw that his IQ test was quite low. He remembered that he was feeling rotten the day of the test.

RELATIONSHIP SKILLS

There are two types of relationship skills. The first type includes your operating relationship skills. Do you like to work on your own or with others? Are you good one-on-one, or are you better in a group? Do you find that you like someone to give you general directions or detailed ones? Are you frequently in positions of leadership or are you a follower?

Include the answers to these questions in your skill list.

The second type is how you relate to others on a day-to-day basis. Working is a social situation, and you must be able to relate to others.

Look at your stories for relationship skills. If you are weak in this area, work on it because your survival in a job will depend on it. When you go to work, you are in a social situation. If this is a problem—and we all need as much help as we can get in this area—read *How to Win Friends and Influence People* by Dale Carnegie. This is the classic book on relationships. When I first heard about it, I thought it was about manipulating people. It is not; it is about relating to people.

In addition to relating one-on-one, you must also know how to work on a team. This applies to white-collar jobs as well as blue-collar jobs. For example, a friend of mine is an industrial electrician and works on large industrial projects. He always works with other people. Sometimes, it is dangerous work, and they must work together.

I just looked at the career Web site for CIBC, a large Canadian bank with operations in Canada and the United States. I wanted to see what skills they wanted in the computer area. Without exception, each job had "ability to work with others" in addition to the relevant computer skills. I also looked at the career section of the General Electric Web site. It was similar and almost every position required the ability to work with others, either informally or on a team. I have a friend who works at Research in Motion, where everyone is a computer expert. Part of his job is to be a team leader. On the teams, they must all work together to solve problems and carry out their work.

VALUES

Lastly, consider your values. I do not want to go into a lot of detail here, but you need to consider what you believe is important in life.

You can find a list of values at www.cdm.uwaterloo.ca. Work through that checklist to help you.

It is also important to think through your ethical values, what you consider to be right or wrong. I know that some people think this is irrelevant, but I disagree. I remember being in a group with a number of friends discussing questions such as "What do you do when your boss asks you to lie about a certain issue?" The other men answered by saying that it was a small city and it was easy to ruin your reputation so you should tell the truth.

Here is an example I heard during a lecture. The assistant to the president of a very large corporation answered the telephone for the president. The caller asked to talk to the president. The president told the assistant to tell the caller that he was not in. What should he do? He did something very risky; he gave the phone to the president and said, "You tell him." As you can imagine, the president was furious. The assistant replied, "If you want me to lie for you, how will you know when I am lying to you?" He kept his job. I am not sure if I could handle that situation so well.

Here is another story about using specific work skills. The attendees at a large management seminar were divided into groups of six or seven and were given a pile of blocks. The contest was to see which team could build the highest tower. At the beginning, they all started to build and were telling each other what to do. There was great confusion in all the groups except one. In that group, one of the men told them that he built towers with his kids all the time; in fact, he was very good at it. So the other members just sat back and let him build the tower. Needless to say, they won the contest.

Make a list of your skills starting with your top skill and working down. Make a list of about ten skills. Then complete the sections on operating relationships, relationship skills, and values.

Donald Ford

Skills Priority List

1.
2.
3.
4.
5.
6.
7.
8.
9.
10.

Operating Relationships

Relationship Skills

Values

Let me give you an illustration of how this can be done. I will use one of my stories.

First, let me give you a little background. For five years during my summer holidays, I was waterfront director at a recreational camp. Then I started working full-time and was made business manager of the camp. This was part of a larger job, and my supervisor was the head of the organization. There was also a camp committee which did not have formal authority but had informal authority. Several years earlier, there had been a major upset at the camp, and as a result, the enrollment was low and many of the buildings were in need of repair.

The first year I ran the camp as best I could and started to think of ways I could improve things. The camp was a mess. It was run by the camp committee chairman who was not on-site. It was physically deteriorating and in financial difficulty. I worked with the committee and gradually took control of the camp. This was a difficult time.

The first thing I did was move the camp office to the campsite.

The first winter, we had a great deal of snow, and as a result, the main building almost completely collapsed. The next spring, we had to rebuild the building. We borrowed large tools which were used in train wrecks from the railway. These were used to push the building into position. We asked an architect who was a friend of the camp to design the roof so that it would withstand future snowfalls.

We worked with a graphic artist, a former camper, to design a logo and letterhead.

I read all the books I could find about camp management and attended camp association meetings to learn how a camp should be operated. This was a big help in running the camp and developing a master plan.

We had well-organized visitors' days to overcome the bad publicity the camp had received. Some prominent doctors, businesspeople, and even the mayor started sending their children to the camp.

In the kitchen, we worked with the cooks to set up menus rather than going from day to day and were able to order food according to the established menus. I had difficulty in hiring cooks because we could not afford to pay much. I developed a multiyear master plan for the physical facilities and had it approved by the camp committee. As a result, we were able to start replacing and relocating the cabins and purchase a new forty-eight-foot all-weather boat and additional canoes. I learned how to operate the boat and received certification from the federal government. I was also an expert canoeist.

I reviewed the insurance policies. I made sure that the camp was ready at the opening date, although some of the committee members complained that we had too many staff come before the campers arrived.

I visited various cities and towns to publicize the camp and recruit staff. My goal was to have the camp full.

Four years later, we had a new boat and additional canoes and about half the old cabins had been replaced. We had an H-shaped swimming dock. The camps were almost full. We also had a first-class out-trip program in place, and our financial position was greatly improved.

From the above, you can see my skills.

Skills with people
- Persuading
- Managing, supervising
- Leading

Skills with information
- Researching
- Organizing
- Improving
- Planning, developing
- Achieving

Skills with things
- Operating the boat

The main challenge for me was working with the camp committee. I often wonder if I tried to make too many changes and was in too much of a hurry. I have difficulty handling conflict in a committee meeting. This is my main weakness.

The above analysis will give you an example of how to develop a skills list. The interesting thing I noticed about myself is that the skills in that list are ones I have always used and the weakness has been there in different settings.

Operating Relationship Skills
I work best if someone in authority gives me general directions. For example, when I started at the college, my job description was: Take the college to the community. So I, in addition to the regular evening classes, started courses in different communities away from the main college campus.

Relationship Skills
I can relate to people quite well on a one-to-one basis, although I have difficulty handling conflict.

Values
I like helping people succeed.

I have tried to show you how to develop your skills list by telling about myself. I encourage you to develop your own list.

YOUR SPECIAL OR TECHNICAL KNOWLEDGE

Your transferable skills are ones you will use on different jobs; your technical skills are the ones you use that are specific to the job and will determine your field of work. For example, accounting, brain surgery, hockey, teaching French, and so on, all require different special or technical knowledge.

By different special knowledge, I mean things like knowledge of plumbing, electrical installation, fiber-glassing boats, and small appliance repair; having the ability to speak Spanish, cook at a professional level, or use Peachtree Complete or Microsoft Dynamics GP accounting programs; or knowing about stock trading, skiing, real estate sales, Internet marketing, copywriting, portrait photography, travel writing, brain anatomy, crane operation, marketing, seismograph interpretation, using steel in construction, planting wheat, dental anatomy, hairstyling, manicuring, and so on.

In the example above, I learned about camp operation. What job skills have you picked up and which can you take with you?

These skills will determine your field of work. It is probably best to stay in your field of work, if possible. Even in today's tough economy, transferable skills will travel with you and can be implemented in different fields. For example, skills used running a doctor's office might transfer easily to working for a health insurance company's call center. If you decide to change your field of work, you must be prepared to learn that field thoroughly and become very competent.

The real estate person I told you about changed from teaching to real estate. She took all the courses and did very well; in fact, as I said before, she got her broker's license and could have set up her own company.

So you now need to make a technical skills list.

In the following charts, list everything you know that could be relevant to working. Circle the ones you enjoy, prioritize, and then pick the top ten. If you need more space, use a separate piece of paper for each section. This exercise is adapted from *The New Quick Job-Hunting Map* by Richard Bowles.

Take your time to do this thoroughly; you will be surprised at how much you know.

These exercises will take from six to ten hours, but remember, you are planning a project that will take a significant part of your life and will bring in an income of at least a million dollars, and in many ways, you are planning your life; so plan well.

Special Knowledge I Picked Up in School or College

Special Knowledge I Picked Up at Work or at Home

Donald Ford

Special Knowledge I Picked Up at Seminars or Workshops

Special Knowledge I Picked Up by Reading or Talking to People

30

Now list your technical or special knowledge and pick the top ten.

1. _____
2. _____
3. _____
4. _____
5. _____
6. _____
7. _____
8. _____
9. _____
10_____

By now, you should have a good idea about what you can do well and enjoy doing. Double-check on the Web site www.occupationalinfo. org to make sure you fit the jobs you are interested in. You will also have an idea of how you relate to people, your ideal operating relationships, and your values.

Share all this information with your mentor.

MUST-HAVE SKILLS

Before going on, there are some skills which you must have; if you are weak in these areas, work on them. Your survival will depend on it. The first three are based on concepts from the Conference Board of Canada.

First, you need a foundation of good communication skills, both written and spoken; a capacity to analyze, evaluate, and solve problems; and the ability to learn new assignments and new ways of doing things when technology changes.

For example, in my story, I told about the building that almost collapsed. This was a major problem. I heard about it from one of our staff who went to the camp in the spring to start getting it open. Fortunately, we had a new staff member who was an expert carpenter. He was able to analyze the situation and decide what to do. We were able to borrow heavy-duty tools used in train wrecks from the railway which we used to push the building back into shape. We had an architect design the roof so that it would stand up under large snow loads.

Second, you need personal management skills such as a positive attitude, the ability to take responsibility and be accountable, the ability to deal with change in the workplace, time management skills, and respect for others.

For example, several years ago, when computers were just being introduced to business, I heard about a man who worked in the collection department of a large company. He was very successful. However, the company was just in the early stages of using computers. He had great difficulty in changing the way he was doing things. He realized that if he wanted to keep his job, he needed to change. He took the necessary training and kept his job.

Third, you need teamwork skills. These skills provide the ability to work with others on a job to achieve the best results. They mean putting the team ahead of your own interests.

In addition, there are three more essential skills you'll need to succeed at any career:

1) The ability to drive a car, even if you do not own one; this is for your own independence and safety
2) Computer literacy
3) Understanding and use of basic statistics

You may be saying "Why statistics?" In many work situations, people will talk about averages, moving averages, exponential moving averages, graphs or histograms, percentages, and probabilities. You must be able to interpret this data at least on an elementary level. I don't mean that you have to become an expert.

If you are going to work in a nonprofit organization such as an industrial board of directors, a church, or a charity, you will need to know how to work with a board and understand how a board works. One of the best books is called *Serving as a Board Member* by Dick L. Kranendonk. This book helps board members and the executive director understand their different roles. It has an interesting subtitle: *Protecting Yourself from Legal Liability While Serving Charities.*

By now, you are probably starting to zero in on a job you would like to do. In the next section, I will show you how to research the job market. Before I do that, I want to say more about weaknesses.

YOUR WEAKNESSES, THINGS THAT COULD DESTROY YOUR CAREER

As I said before, it is essential that you know your weaknesses as they relate to your work; these are the things that can hold you back or even destroy your career. As you have thought about yourself and your work, think about your weaknesses. This could be your relationships with people, your inability to handle ideas, or your inability to handle things. With many people, words are what cause difficulties. Words can build up or tear people down.

A man we will call Stewart was very successful in running a nonprofit agency; he was able to raise large amounts of money, recruit excellent board members, and develop plans. However, he had one major weakness which the board became aware of; every once in a while, he would rip into a staff member and use words to almost destroy the person. The board chair talked to him about this situation but was unable to get him to change. Finally, they had to let him go before he did any more damage.

Here are some specific examples of potential challenges in a variety of occupations. If you can't handle these issues, that will be a weakness for you:

- A nurse has to be able to do his or her job as a nurse; however, nursing also involves handling patients who can be physically violent.
- Anyone dealing with the public will from time to time have strange or very obnoxious customers.
- A real estate representative sometimes has to deal with dishonest people.
- I ran a summer camp but part of the job was dealing with a camp committee.
- Sometimes, your job involves working with a supervisor who is incompetent.
- A small businessperson could be very competent in the export/import business but not do well at record keeping.
- Working in a not-for-profit organization can be very gratifying; however, in many organizations, you will also be expected to do a lot of fund-raising.
- Consultants like to help people or organizations, but part of the job includes finding customers.
- You may operate the best bed-and-breakfast in town, but you will not be successful unless you do a lot of marketing.
- You could be an expert in computer operation and application, but part of the job is working on a team. I was surprised to see the emphasis placed on this while looking at job descriptions in the computer area.
- I often look at the credits at the end of a motion picture. It never ceases to amaze me that the producers and directors

are able to get all these creative people to work together. They are all very creative and probably high-strung, but they all must work together to produce the picture.

Be aware of these things, and when you apply for a job, decide if you can overcome your weak areas. It is part of the job, and in some cases, you have to do things you are not good at. The only way is to take training. For some people, their weaknesses become their strengths.

Take some time to write out your weaknesses. Be realistic, but don't be too hard on yourself. Be conscious of things you do that might hurt your career prospects.

My Weaknesses in Relation to People

My Weaknesses in Relation to Ideas or Information

My Weaknesses in Relation to Things

You're already on your way to controlling your career. Here's what you've learned so far:

- Transferable skills with people, data, and tools move with you from one job to another.
- By reviewing your past accomplishments and using various resources to explore the job market, you can discover your skills and be prepared for job changes.
- Relationship skills encompass your abilities to work with various types of people.
- Your values are a factor in your career field.
- Your special or technical knowledge comes through education and job experience.
- The "must-have" skills needed for all types of jobs and careers are communication skills, management skills, teamwork skills, computer literacy, ability to drive a car, and understanding of basic statistics.
- Your weaknesses are gaps in knowledge or behavior issues that could wreck your career.

Now that you have a good idea of your skills—transferable, relationship, and technical—and what you would like to do with them, let's move on to the next chapter, which shows you how to research the job market.

Chapter Three

Where Do You Want to Work?

Now that you have a good idea of what you can do well and enjoy doing, as well as areas where you are weak, the big question is: "Where will I work?" In this section, you will find answers to five questions.

1. How do I research the job market?
2. How do I select job targets to investigate?
3. How can I make sure I will fit a position?
4. Where do I get information about different positions?
5. Are self-employment and part-time business good options?
6. How do I go about goal setting?

How Do You Research the Job Market?

You research the job market by looking at the countrywide picture and then narrowing it down to your province, state, or local authority. These pictures give you broad trends and show where jobs are in your country. In these difficult times, it may be that you need to consider relocation.

This section is divided into three subsections: the first dealing with Canada, the second with the United States, and the third with methods that work in both countries. In each section, I will start with the big picture and then narrow it down to a local one.

Searching the Job Market in Canada

The first step is to look at the Canadian federal government Web site dealing with employment. It is www.servicecanada.ca. Then go down the left to "Employment" and scroll down to "Life Events," "Looking for a Job," and "Job Search." You will also find a site called "Job Bank," which lists most of the jobs available in Canada.

In addition, this site has useful information for newcomers to Canada, aboriginal people, people with disabilities, and veterans and information about self-employment, income support, and training.

You can also go to your local Service Canada Office, and they can tell you about jobs all over Canada as well as in your local area.

Your province will also have useful information. For example, the Web site for Ontario is www.ontariojobfutures.ca. It will give you a wealth of information on jobs in Ontario, future trends, and job descriptions. Spend some time on this site; much of it is applicable to other jurisdictions, especially the job descriptions. The part dealing with trends starts with 2004 which is quite out of date; however, scroll down to trends in 2009, and it will give up-to-date projections.

You can also put the name of a job in the box on the left, and it will give you a job description, educational requirements, and future trends.

Other provinces have similar Web sites; on Google, put in "employment in ..."

There are a number of Web sites listing jobs. Here are four:

www.monster.ca

www.workopolis.com

www.jobbank.ca

www.careerbuilder.ca

Look up "employment Web sites in Canada" on Google for more Web sites.

You should also look at www.weddles.com and read all it says in the section "Tips for Success." It tells you how to apply for a job that has been listed on a Web site.

Searching the Job Market in the United States

The USA Web site is www.occupationalinfo.org. Click on "Dictionary of Occupational Titles." Go to "Table of Contents." Click on the occupation you are interested in. This will give you information about jobs. This is useful for American workers or for people who want to work in the USA.

The United States federal government Web site relating to employment statistics is www.bls.gov/home.htm. This site contains an amazing amount of information; simply click on the section you are interested in. The most helpful links are "Wages, Earnings, & Benefits," "Occupations," "Employment & Unemployment," "Industries," "Geography," and "Kids' Stuff." The last one, in spite of the heading, will be very helpful for high school and college students.

If you want information about a specific state or city, go to Google. For example, put in "employment in Chicago," and you will find dozens of responses.

States will have similar information. Try keywords such as "employment in New York." There is a lot of information. I did it with other states and got similar results. If you add in "state," as in "New York State," you will get list of government positions.

There are many job Web sites. One of the best ways to find them is to go to www.weddles.com and click on "User's Choice Awards"; this a list of the top thirty job sites as voted by the users. Look at the section called "Tips for Success." Read everything he has listed, and you will know how to apply for a job using an online job site.

American readers or people who want to work in the U.S. can look on Google under "job search in USA." You will find a large number of options. Or you can use any country or city in the world; simply put "job search in ..."

Some of these pages will also give you ideas about self-employment and franchises.

However, realize that many jobs are not advertised. This is called the hidden job market. I talk more about that in the next section, "General Job Search Methods."

General Job Search Methods

There are also more general ways to search for a job, which will apply no matter where you live. Keep in mind that many jobs are not advertised, so you have to find these jobs on your own. I will show you how to do that.

The city where you live or where you want to live will have an economic development office, which will give a picture of your area of interest. They will give you a list of local employers, trends, and information about your area. You can find this information about other cities you are interested in. Make an appointment with one of their staff to get a better picture of what is available.

In addition, the chamber of commerce in your area will have a list of members. From that, you can see which companies interest you. You will probably find employers you have never heard of before on their list. Well-run small companies are often good places to work. If you are a member of a union, you may find that jobs in the area are handled by them.

If you have completed an apprentice program, either the apprenticeship training group will help you or if it is unionized, the union will help.

As I said, many jobs are not posted and you have to find them yourself. Have your résumé with you all the time. Give one to everyone you know and tell them you are looking for work. (In the next chapter, I tell you how to create a strong résumé.)

Another way is to drive around, and if you see someplace that looks interesting, stop and find out if they are hiring people. Leave your résumé with them and ask them to get in touch when they have an opening.

Also, many companies are members of professional associations or trade organizations. Contact them for possible openings too.

In addition, many companies list career opportunities on their Web site. Simply go to Google and put in "careers at [name of company]." These companies will list the positions available along with a job description and skills needed. It will also tell how to apply for the position. Some will tell you what they want in a résumé and how to conduct yourself in an interview. It is important to follow these instructions to the letter; otherwise, your résumé will not be read. A computer will probably be the first to read your résumé and will be looking for keywords.

As I said earlier, a very useful Web page is www.weddles.com. It gives advice about finding a job using the Internet. Follow his "Tips for Success when Looking for a Better Job on the Internet." While it is directed at American job seekers, much of the advice is applicable to Canadians as well.

Please note that if you are ready to apply for a job and you are using the Internet, you must follow their instructions exactly. The sites will tell you how to apply, so do exactly as they say, or your application will not be read. I talk more about applying for a job in the next section.

You can also go to Google and enter "job opportunities in [your field]." For example, you might be interested in photography. So you look for "jobs in photography" on Google. You will also find all sorts of information about job searches and a wide variety of Web pages.

Asking friends or networking is probably the best way to research the job market. Tell all your friends and business associates about the kind of job you are looking for; often, they will know of a place that is looking for someone like you. It is like fishing; the wider you spread your net, the more likely you are to catch a fish. This is called networking. Everywhere you go, have some résumés and give them out. Be sure the résumé is up-to-date.

Another way is to look for companies in the yellow pages in your telephone book. Contact them and ask if they are hiring people with your skills.

If you can't find anything in your area, drive to different cities. If you are married, with your wife or husband, decide together where you would like to live and work. Look at the schools, community activities, shopping, and churches. Talk to people to find out what it is like. Ask, "Would we like to live here?"

Newspaper and trade association job advertisements are another source of positions. However, some organizations are required by law or company policy to advertise open positions. They may already have the candidate they are looking for; in which case, you could be wasting your time. Be especially careful about answering advertisements placed by your own company. Sometimes companies do this to find out who is looking around. If a company posts a job internally and externally, you could be free to apply; if it is only posted externally, you could talk to human resources to find out if it is filled or not.

SELECTING JOB TARGETS

At some stage, you will need to select at least two job targets. Ask yourself, "Where do I want to be in three to five years or even eight to ten years." Then decide on immediate and intermediate steps to achieve your goal. Answers to these questions will help you focus on where you are going and give you a sense of direction. They will also help you with intermediate goals. They may seem like long-range goals, but when you look back, you realize it is really not a very long time. Here is a word from one of my mentors. He said we tend to overemphasize what we can do in one year and underemphasize what we can do in five years.

> ✓ Case Study: Stewart
> Here is an example of a real-life career progression. Stewart Hall graduated with a BA in business. His first job for a large organization was at a beginning level; he was given the assignment of turning a parking garage from a losing enterprise into a profitable, or at least a break-even, operation. Over a period of a year, he was able to turn it around. This success helped him to learn that he had the ability to use his accounting skills to improve an operation. He then went on and earned an advanced degree in accounting. He now works for a company that owns twenty-six smaller companies; some are profitable, and some are not. He is comptroller and is working on turning all the smaller companies into profitable ones.

Here is an example of planning ahead. Let's say a person wanted to own his or her own plumbing company. The steps would be:
1. get a job as a plumber
2. complete the plumber apprenticeship program
3. keep working as a plumber
4. complete a small business course
5. start a small plumbing company

6. as it grows, hire other people

Try it for yourself. Decide on a target job and then plan out the immediate and intermediate steps to reach that goal:

Job target #1
    1.
    2.
    3.
    4.
    5.
    6.

Job target #2
    1.
    2.
    3.
    4.
    5.
    6.

This should give you a feel for what tasks you need to start on right away and which will be longer term tasks. It's helpful to have a road map for where you're going no matter what your goal is.

MAKING SURE YOU WILL FIT THE PROPOSED POSITION

In addition to knowing what skills are needed in the new position, you need to look at your people preferences. Sometimes you can't do anything about this, but before applying or accepting a position, take a long, hard look at what is called people preferences.

Look at the following charts. In the first, make a list of the characteristics of people who drain your energy. In the second, make a list of the characteristics of people you like to work with or for. Some people have thick skin and can work in any situation; others can't. There is a copy at the back for you to photocopy.

I know a person who was quite successful and did a great job. Instead of encouraging the person, her boss always found something wrong. This really got to her, and finally, she left. She later said that the old company had a poisoned atmosphere for her. Other people got along just fine. So these are subjective characteristics.

When you are doing your research, decide if this situation will drain you or will be more in line with your people preferences and will help you grow.

Write down the things in the first chart that might drain you, and in the second, write down things that will help you grow in the position.

Sometimes, you can't do anything about it, so learn to live with it. Working with difficult people can also make you stronger. It is important to know what you are getting into.

PEOPLE PREFERENCES CHART

Characteristics of People Who Drain Me

Characteristics of People Who Help Me Grow and Develop

Four Ways to Research Different Jobs

You can research a position in four ways:
- reading,
- talking to people,
- shadowing, and
- information interviews.

The first way, if you are employed, is to look at the job description manual in your company and read about what the department does. As you look at the different positions, you will start seeing potential jobs from your list. If you are looking outside your present employer, look on the Web site of the company you are interested in; this will have job descriptions. You will also find books in the library outlining different occupations. Another way is to look at the Web sites mentioned at the beginning of this chapter. The one I find most helpful is www. occupationalinfo.org. Go to "Contents" and find the job description, or go to "ONET"; it also has job descriptions.

The second way is to talk to people who do the kind of work you are interested in. They may be in your organization or employed with another company.

The third way is to shadow. You will need to get permission to spend time in the department or company simply watching what is happening. Let me give a personal example. I was interested in a small business franchise that was engaged in finding people who were interested in changing jobs; this is commonly called "headhunting." They invited me to spend some time in the office watching what a headhunter did all day. He spent all day on the telephone trying to find people who might be interested in changing jobs; to be honest, I found this to be very boring. At the end of the day, I decided this job was not for me, thanked the people, and left.

The fourth way is the information interview. Do this once you have done some reading and know something about the position. The purpose is to find out firsthand what the job is all about. Make an appointment with a manager or person who has a job like the one you are interested in and conduct the interview over coffee or in the manager's office.

An information interview can sometimes lead to a job offer.

Below is a checklist of the kind of information you want to get.

Objectives of Information Interviews
1. Find out what the major responsibilities are and which major skills are required.
2. Find out what the department is like.
3. Find out what the people are like.
4. Find out about compensation.

Possible Questions
1. What skills are required, both transferable and technical?
2. What special projects need doing?
3. How can I get a job here?
4. What skills are most important?
5. What is most rewarding? Most frustrating?
6. What training is required? Are there possibilities for growth?
7. What is the degree of supervision?
8. How are employees evaluated?
9. Would it use these skills, (list yours)?
10. How much experience is needed? Who else could I talk to?

Use this form to keep track of your interviews. Be sure to follow up with a thank-you note.

Example of an Information Interview Record

Information Interview Record

Date: September 10, 2009 Name of person interviewed: Susan Davis

Telephone: 436-8326 E-mail: sdavis@abc.com

Position: Sales supervisor

Names of others in the department: Bruce Fulton, Roger James

What was said:
Could use my skills in sales, many have similar skills
People are aggressive, egocentric, will take your prospects, competitive
 Boss is excellent, sets high standards

What skills are needed:
 Verbal ability
 Detail, follow-through
 Negotiating ability
 Work one-on-one
Date of thank-you note sent. (Make sure you have the correct spelling of the person's name and it is typed.) September 20, 2009

Information Interview Record (See also the sample in the Appendix for photocopying)

Date: _____ Name: _____

Telephone: _____ E-mail: _____

Position: _____ Department: _____

Names of others in the department: _____

What was said _____
_____
_____
_____

What skills are needed _____
_____
_____
_____

Date of thank-you note sent. (Make sure you have the correct spelling of the person's name and it is typed.)

SELF-EMPLOYMENT OR PART-TIME BUSINESS

In the current economic climate, many people will need to look at self-employment as an option. This is not detailed information, but I decided to say a few words because of its importance, especially at this time.

For example, Beth Saunders aged forty-five or so, worked as a graphic designer for one of the local newspapers. The new owners decided to farm out all the graphic design work, and Beth was laid off. She had skills in that area and a lot of contacts; she started her own graphic business and after a slow start is doing very well.

Another example is Andrew Sloan, aged fifty-five, who was the comptroller in a medium-sized company. A new president was hired, and he dismissed all the former senior staff. Andrew decided to set up his own accounting practice. He was already well-known in the accounting association and after a slow start the first year was able to get his practice established.

In addition to researching different positions in your organization and looking at different companies, you might want to take a good look at self-employment. Some people would say that you should always have a part-time business in addition to your regular job for three reasons.

- First, you never know when your regular job will finish and you will be unemployed. This part-time business will enable you to keep your financial head above water. If circumstances permit, you could also use this time to develop your business into a full-time job.
- Second, a small business has tax benefits. You will be able to deduct many expenses from your business income.
- Finally, there is a whole school of thought called multiple sources of income. One source could dry up or be seasonal. If you have other sources, you can still function financially. Most businesses have multiple streams of income and rarely rely on one product. For example, a gardening business is seasonal and can be combined with snowplowing in the winter.

Here is an example: Susan Harris has four sources of income. She is a travel writer, copywriter, author of a course on travel writing, and seminar leader on travel writing; she conducts her business from home. Note that the separate businesses are all related. Her copywriting job deals with the tourism industry.

Here are some thoughts for you to consider.

First, you must have adequate resources, whatever that may be, such as a computer, telephone, and so on. If you are in a family setting, remind everyone that this is for business purposes only.

You need financial resources as well. Resources also include training so that you know what you are doing. In other words, know the business thoroughly.

Second, develop a business plan. There are books and courses to show you how to do this. In my opinion, the most important thing is to set goals that are achievable, measurable, and within your budget. At the same time, they should stretch you.

Third, this is a business, not a hobby. Keep regular hours, have a place to work, and ask others in the house to respect this. Also, make yourself accountable to your mentor who will keep you on track. Everyone needs a boss. Finally, review and revise your goals every three months and look for ways to improve your performance; in other words, adopt a plan of continuous improvement.

Fourth, control your emotions. These include greed, discouragement, and fear of failure. These are the three killers.

Fifth, be patient. It might take up to three years to get up to speed. Do not quit your regular job but work on the part-time one until you have replaced your income.

The Canadian and American governments have excellent Web sites to help you start your own business. The Canadian site is www.canadabusiness.ca and the American site is www.usa.gov/Business/Self_Employed.

The United States' site has information about financial assistance, franchises, getting started, hiring, laws and regulations, licensing, retirement plans, scams and fraud, Social Security and Medicare, and taxes. Each section opens up to more information.

In Canada, start with the "Canada Business" site, and then go to "Starting a Business" and from there "Business Startup Assistant." This page is a table of contents for all the information.

Much of the information is applicable to both countries except the taxes and government regulations.

There are numerous sources of ideas. Be sure to check them carefully to make sure they will help you achieve your goals.

Enter "self-employment in the United States" or "self-employment in Canada" on Google. This will return a large number of Web sites.

Here are three sources of information that may interest you. First, if you are interested in learning how to make money with stock options or the stock market, look at www.onlineoption.com. If you are interested in making money by copywriting, Internet marketing, travel writing, photography, or graphic design, look at www.DirectResponseJobs.com. Third, the Self-Council Press has books for small businesses; it has American and Canadian offices and books. Its Web page is www.self-counsel.com.

If you are a work-at-home parent, take a look at www.themompreneur.com.

Here is another example: About ten years ago, Stan Grant was laid off because of a downturn in his company. He looked for similar work, but all the other companies in his field were also laying off employees. He had very strong technical abilities, and with borrowed money, working in his basement for long hours, he designed and built specialized electronic equipment. His former company had built similar equipment, and so he had the technical skills and knowledge to do so. His equipment reduces costs and is in demand. His self-employment has turned into a company that employs over fifty people.

From time to time, we need things fixed at our home. For example, at my home, the drain to the outside got plugged and the basement started to flood with raw sewage; that called for quick action. We called the plumber, and for a fee of $125.00, he opened up the drain. He was self-employed.

Now let me give you a word of caution. Be sure to exercise due diligence before purchasing an expensive course or system. Ask for references. Check everyone out.

SUMMARY OF THINGS TO DO TO RESEARCH A POSITION

In addition to the things we have discussed, there are a number of other aspects that you need to take into consideration before accepting a position or making a change. This information is adapted from *The Job Search Companion* by Ellen J. Wallach and Peter Arnold. I have left a few blank lines on which you can make notes. In addition, there is a copy of this form in the back for photocopying.

In view of the current economic situation, it is absolutely essential that you determine the financial strength of the company you want to work for. If the company is a publicly traded company, you can look it up in your bank investment section. If you have trouble understanding the numbers, ask at your bank or other financial institution or ask a friend who may be knowledgeable and able to find out the information you need. You do not want to get on a sinking ship. If the company is not publicly listed, ask at the chamber of commerce or other source about the company.

These are the items to check when researching a position.

1. Skills—Ask yourself, "Does this use most of my preferred skills?" Avoid underemployment if at all possible. Challenge yourself. Also ask, "What of my weakness? Can I handle this job? What do I need to work on?" _____

_____

_____

_____

_____

_____

Often, you will find that there are a lot of sales jobs. During the interview, they will assure you that anyone can sell or the product or service will sell itself. The only way to know is to try. Give it your best shot. If you can sell, keep going. If not, get a job that uses your skills.

If you are a student, use your vacation or co-op work term to try different jobs and learn what your skills are. You probably have all sorts of hidden talents that you did not know about. This is also an excellent time to explore different industries or fields of work.

A friend of mine felt that he would like to work in North Africa, so he worked there during his summer vacation. He wanted to see if he could work in that environment. This was an excellent experience for him; he liked the organization, the country, and the work but decided that he could not work in that situation. He decided against it and joined another similar organization where after several years he became president.

2. Supervisor—Ask yourself, "Could I really work for this person? Is there respect, acceptance, appreciation, and chemistry?" Be assured that you are also being sized up by your interviewer. _____

_____

_____

_____

_____

_____

3. People in the department—Ask yourself, "Can I work with these people? Are there a lot of people who turn me off?" Don't shy away from such people; sometimes people who are energy drainers can help you grow and mature and make you stronger.

_____

_____

_____

_____

_____

_____

4. The new department or company—Ask yourself, "Is the department or company conservative and cautious, or are they risk takers? Is the company profitable, growing, declining, turning around, or facing difficulties?" As I said before, it is essential that you find out the financial health of the company. ____

_____

_____

_____

_____

How does the department relate to the total organization? _____

_____

_____

_____

_____

What about working conditions and things like technical support? _____

_____

_____

_____

_____

Does this company fit your life goals? For example, if the goods, services, treatment of suppliers and employees, and practices of the company are incompatible with your ethical or moral standards, you need to think twice about working there. _____

_____

_____

_____

5. Compensation package—Look at things like basic salary, bonuses, and benefits. Does it fit your level of aspirations? _____

_____

_____

_____

_____

6. Potential for personal growth—Will this position enable you to grow and to reach your targeted position? Does it relate to your stage in life? I have a chart showing the various career stages in life at the end of this section. Is it a dead-end or a flow-through job? Are there training and development opportunities?

_____

_____

_____

_____

_____

7. Shift work or hours expected—Does this job have a regular shift, changing shift, or standard hours? Does this fit in with your family? _____

_____

_____

_____

_____

_____

8. Geography—How far do you have to commute? I have heard it said that you should try to live within a one-hour commute to work. Decide how far you want to go, get a map, and draw a circle out as far as you want to go. Look for jobs within that circle. Do you need to move? How far? Again, how will this fit in with your family? Also, if you have to commute, get the most comfortable car you can afford. Get some learning CDs.

_____

_____

_____

_____

There are many factors to consider. Spend time thinking about the different issues. You might want to put a weight on each one. Some items may not apply to you or you may not think they are important. They will help you make a decision. Again, try to get at least two targets.

Edward Schein has written a book called *Career Dynamics* which relates careers to organizational needs. In the first section, he shows how careers relate to the various stages a person passes through in his or her life. Here is a summary of some of his main ideas.

Life Stages		
Stage	Characteristics	Age
1.	Growth, fantasy, exploration	0–21
2.	Entry into the world of work	16–25
3.	Basic training	16–25
4.	Early career	17–30
5.	Mid career	25+
6.	Mid-career transition or crisis	35–45
7.	Late career in non-leadership role	40+
8.	Late career in leadership role	40+
9.	Decline and disengagement	40+
10.	Retirement	65+

You can see from the list above how life stages have a direct impact on your career and goals. These are concepts to keep in mind when planning.

GOAL SETTING

Here is the old question: "How do you eat an elephant?" The answer is "One bite at a time." You take your goal and then break it down into smaller pieces.

Definition of a goal: A goal is a statement of measurable results to be achieved. It translates dreams into reality, lets you know when you win, and is tangible and reality oriented.

Qualities of a Goal. A goal is:
- Specific
- Timed, accomplished by a certain date
- Relevant to your abilities or position in the organization
- Attainable, will stretch you but is not impossible. Most non-achievers set impossible goals and then give up when they are not achieved.
- Measurable, this depends on the goal. This could be income earned, percent quality product, marks in a course, date completing a course, and so on.
- It is short and simple.

Model of a Goal: to (action or single measurable result) by (target date) at (cost)

For example, you travel a lot and decide that you are going to sell some of your photographs and help pay for your trip to France which is about six months away.

Here is your goal statement.

By August 2009, sell $1,000.00 worth of photographs at a cost of $400.00 for training. You decide to use the equipment you have.

You bought a photography course which shows how to take saleable photos and how to sell them. The course has fifty-eight chapters. One approach would be to master two chapters a week so that by next summer, you are ready to earn income as a travel photographer.

The next step is to make a step-by-step plan showing the chapter headings and date completed, as in the following example.

Chapter	Date completed
Chapters 1 and 2	January 30
Chapters 3 and 4	February 2

The important thing is to concentrate on key result areas. These are things that will make a difference.

It is important that you write these goals down and read them every day. This will help you keep focused and achieve your goals.

Here is an exercise for you to work on.

Select three, three-to-five-year goals and write them in the form of goal statements which include a single measurable result, target date, and cost. After an investigation, boil this down to two goals.

Say to yourself: What would I like to be working at three-to-five years from now?

Here are two sample goals.

Example One:
By June 2011, be employed as a bilingual executive secretary at a cost of $550.00 for training.

Step one: enroll in language class and pay tuition	within 45 days
Step two: attend classes for one semester	within 4 months
Step three: approach supervisor and ask for more responsibility	within 6 months
Step four: etc.	

Example Two:
By December 2012, have a house-building business established and build 10 houses each year which sell for $300,000.

Step one: investigate classes for contractor's license	within 30 days
Step two: enroll in class and pay tuition	within 3 months
Step three: explore equipment needed for business, get quotes	within 6 months
Step four: draft business plan and start search for capital funding	within 12 months
Step five: etc.	

Your goals:
Goal #1 (Remember, it must be specific, time-oriented, and measurable.)

Step one: _____

Step two: _____

Step three: _____

Step four: _____

Goal #2

Step one: _____

Step two: _____

Step three: _____

Step four: _____

Goal #3

Step one: _____

Step two: _____

Step three: _____

Step four: _____

You've already accomplished a great deal in your career plan! Here's what you've learned so far:

- Researching the job market involves using Internet resources, government agency information, and professional and trade association information; networking with schools, family, and friends; and approaching companies cold.
- Selecting job targets is an important part of your strategy.
- You've analyzed your skills to make sure you will fit the proposed position.
- Getting information about different positions includes online research and interviewing people at various companies.
- You've learned how to set specific, measurable, and attainable goals; and you've developed at least two goals to work on.

Let's move on to getting the job you want.

CHAPTER FOUR

HOW CAN YOU GET THE JOB YOU WANT?

In the previous sections, we talked about self-assessment, career options, career targets, evaluating jobs, and finding information. Now how do we get the job we really want?

In this section, I will show you how to develop a comprehensive career plan, how to develop short- and long-term goals, how to make cover letters and résumés, and how to conduct yourself in a job interview.

COMPREHENSIVE CAREER PLAN

Now that you have completed your skills inventory, researched the market, and decided on two goals, you need to develop a comprehensive career plan that shows where you have been and where you want to go in the future. Let's start with the comprehensive plan. It has been adapted from *Career Management in Organizations* by Elmer H. Burack and Nicholas Mathys.

This plan is like a road map that will help you first to take a look at where you have been and what you have learned and then decide where you want to go in the future and how to get there. In my opinion, this is one of the most important charts in this book.

Look at the Career Planning Worksheet. We will name the employee Sally. The first copy is an example of how to do it. Along the bottom are years starting four years ago. The middle line is today, and the future is projected four years.

The top left section shows where she has been, listing the jobs and/ or schools attended, and work experience. In our example, the person attended high school and then started to work and has had the same position for three years.

The bottom left section lists the relevant training she obtained while at high school and at work. Notice that she picked up very relevant skills while working, such as company knowledge and working with people.

In the top right section, you can see the two jobs she decides that she wants. The first is a correspondence representative position and the second is the position of secretary moving on to executive secretary.

The bottom right section shows the training she needs to take in order for her to move into these positions. This includes accounting, time management, grooming, and so on. This is the head office of a Canadian company, so she decides to learn French.

Complete the plan yourself.

These charts show four years along the bottom. It may be that you want to make the time periods longer, especially going back. Going forward, you will probably keep the time frame at four years. Mark the date at the middle line.

In the top left quarter, start with the schools and colleges you attended and the companies you worked for. Put the positions in the appropriate spaces according to the dates.

Then, in the bottom left quarter, put other training and development activities on the left side. Then put in general terms the skills developed. This will give you a good picture of your past and provide a foundation on which to build your future. As you do this, you will be surprised at what you know and are able to do.

The right side of the chart looks to the future. Show the two positions you have chosen and when you will be ready to move. With Sally, she took two steps to achieve her four-year goal. Think about what job progression you need to plan for. The bottom left section shows the training and development activities you need to undertake to achieve your goal.

Review and revise your plan quarterly to make sure you are on track. Cut it out and put it on the wall to help keep you going on this exciting adventure.

Adapted from "Career Management in Organizations"

Career Planning Worksheet

	−4	−3	−2	−1	0 TODAY	+1	+2	+3	+4
			4 YEARS PAST				4 YEARS FUTURE		
Jobs 1. HIGH SCHOOL	STUDENT →					CORRESPONDENCE REP II →			CORRESPONDENCE REP I →
2. ACME CO.		→	RECEPTIONIST						
3. ACME CO.					SECRETARY →				
4. ACME CO.							EXECUTIVE SECRETARY →		
Outside courses and programs		HIGH SCHOOL →		• WRITING	• WORD PROCESSING	• ACCOUNTING	• FINANCE	• EXECUTIVE SECRETARY WORKSHOP	• FRENCH LANGUAGE
Training ACME CO.						• TIME MANAGEMENT			
Other						• GROOMING			
Skills required or to be acquired	• TYPING • DICTATION • CLERICAL	• COMPANY KNOWLEDGE	• DEALING WITH PEOPLE			• PAPER HANDLING • APPEARANCE		• LANGUAGE – VERBAL LEVEL	

Sample Career Planning Worksheet

Donald Ford

Career Planning Worksheet

Adapted from "Career Management in Organizations"

	−4	−3	−2	−1	0	+1	+2	+3	+4
Jobs 1.									
2.									
3.									
4.									
Outside courses and programs									
Training									
Other									
Skills required or to be acquired									

4 YEARS PAST — TODAY — 4 YEARS FUTURE

SHORT-TERM ACTION PLAN

The next step is a short-term action plan. Once you have decided where you want to go, you need to decide how to get there. That is where this plan comes in.

A blank copy which you can photocopy is in the back of the book. This is your plan for the next six months. Look at the sample plan. Your name goes on top and then the goal or objective. Note that it is quite simple and measurable.

The first column lists the action; the second, who is responsible; the third, the target date; the fourth, the amount of time; the fifth, how much it will cost; and finally, the completion date in the last column. This may seem like a lot of work, but it will be worth the effort. Be sure to show your plan to the person to whom you are responsible or your mentor.

Here I have a partially completed sample plan for Susan Davis who has a junior secretarial position but wants to move into a better position.

Short-Term Action Plan

Name: Susan Davis   Date: June 27/09

Goal: To prepare for move as a bilingual secretary by September 30/09

Action	Who	Target Date	Time	Cost	Date Completed
Check continuing ed programs at Seneca College	Me	July 15	1 hour	NC	
Check into time management training	Me	July 15	15 min	NC	
Check into grooming courses	Me	July 15	15 min	NC	
Check into French training	Me	August 15			

PERSONAL-NEEDS ASSESSMENT

Another way to work on your needs is to develop a personal needs assessment worksheet. This helps you to zero in on the specific skills needed for your next position. Note that you need to put in two targeted positions and the date you will be ready for a transfer, promotion, or an outside job.

The first column lists the required skills and special knowledge. In the next column, you rate yourself. In the third column, you say whether the skill will be required now and/or in the future. The last two columns list the developmental activity or training needed. Here is a sample; a blank form which you can photocopy is in the back of this book.

Personal-Needs Assessment Worksheet

Name: George Clark   Date: June 1, 2009

Current Position:
Receptionist Sales Department

Targeted Position #1:
Sales Representative   Ready Date: December 31, 2009

Targeted Position #2:
Executive Secretary   Ready Date: June 1, 2010

Required Skills or Specialized Knowledge	Rating 1 low 5 high	Required: Now X Future O	Development Activity Needed	Training Needed
Product Knowledge	4	X O		
Computer Skills	5	X O		
Accounting	1	O		Accounting 101 at Seneca College
Conversational Spanish	1	O		Spanish class at Texas College
Time Management	2	O	3-day in-house training	
Continue as needed				

Donald Ford

Different Ways to Apply for a Job

Now, at last, you will say you are ready to apply for one of your targeted jobs. By now, you know yourself quite well and what is required in the new position. So let's move on. There are four ways to apply for a job:
1. Apply for an internal position within your company
2. Apply in person to the new company
3. Apply via the Internet
4. Apply by mail

At the end of this chapter, I will show you how to make a cover letter and a résumé and how to conduct yourself on an interview.

Internal Application

The first way is an internal application. Many companies post new positions; if the desired position is in your company, you will need to follow the established procedure. This will involve filling out an application form and completing a job interview. My recommendation is to make a résumé. You have probably accomplished a lot, so make an up-to-date résumé. It may include things not listed on the application form.

Apply in Person

The second way to apply for a job is to go directly to the company you want to work for and either ask to see the person who makes the hiring decisions or go to the personnel office and tell them what you are interested in doing for them. Many jobs are not advertised; it is called the hidden job market. Also, they may be so impressed with your initiative or with you that they call you in for an interview and create a position for you.

You might also consider telephoning the company to see if there are any positions open in your field of work.

I recently heard about two people who applied for jobs directly. The first was a fifteen-year-old high-school student who wanted to work at the local supermarket. The first time he went in, they were not interested. So he went back every day until they hired him.

The second was a young man who had two jobs. He was getting tired of working all the time. He decided where he wanted to work and sent in a résumé. He waited a few days and then started phoning. He phoned on his morning coffee break, at noon, and then on his afternoon coffee break. He phoned every day until he found out the name of the person who did the hiring. So he started phoning him three times a day. Finally, the manager got so mad that he said, "Okay, start right now!" I am sure he added a few colorful expletives. My friend was already working, so he started the new job the next day. He now has a senior position in that company.

Apply via the Internet

The third way is via the Internet. You will find these jobs listed on the different Web sites listed in the previous section or on company Web sites. You simply follow the directions. Be sure to do exactly what they ask you to do. Your invitation to attend an interview will depend on your compliance. Keep in mind that because of the large number of applicants, a computer will sort the applications, and it will be looking for certain keywords; these keywords are ones in the job description. Each company has its own language, so use this language in your résumé and cover letter.

I give you detailed directions about how to submit a résumé that will be read by a computer in the section about résumés.

Apply Directly by Mail or E-mail

Finally, you may choose to apply directly to the company by mail or e-mail. You must send a cover letter and a résumé. I will tell you how to do that. First, I discuss the cover letter and then traditional résumés. Then, I talk about how to prepare a scannable résumé.

WRITING COVER LETTERS AND RÉSUMÉS

Cover Letters

When you send a résumé, you must accompany it with a cover letter. The only purpose of the letter is to get your prospective employer to read your résumé and ask you for an interview. Let me show you how this is done.

The cover letter should be brief; it summarizes your main qualifications related to the job. In other words, it shows that you are the person they are looking for. Finally, it asks for an interview.

Make sure you have the correct spelling of the recipient's name, job title, company, and address. It should be typed perfectly. Use standard white business paper.

If you need help, go to a secretarial service or a friend who is an expert. Remember the old adage: "You only have one chance to make a first impression." If you make a mistake in any of these items, your letter will not be read and will be thrown into the recycle bin. It is especially important that you spell the name correctly; most people are insulted if you spell their name wrong. Double-check it.

You want the letter to go to the person who makes the hiring decisions. If you don't know who that is, phone the company or talk to a friend who works there and find out. You want the first name, last name, and specific job title. Many women prefer Ms.; some don't, so try to find out.

If you are not able to find this information, use "Dear Sir or Madam."

The first paragraph should make a connection with how you heard about the job. Refer to a newspaper advertisement or some contact you had. For example, several years ago, I saw an article in a newspaper that attracted my attention, and I wanted to work there. So I wrote to the president, and a few days later, I got a call asking me to come for an interview. I referred to the article in the paper in the first paragraph.

Another way to start is to refer to someone who works in the company. Let's say you heard about the job from someone in the company; make sure he or she is a good employee. In your first sentence, start with "Shirley Smith suggested that I contact you about an accounting position open in your department."

These are ways to establish contact with a person. The hoped-for response is that if Shirley Smith made a recommendation, the person must be good.

I know that some organizations encourage staff to make recommendations and will even give a signing bonus.

The next paragraph is the body of your letter. It answers the question, "Why should I read this person's résumé?" You show how your qualifications fit the position. You should pick out three or four of your strongest qualifications.

Use headings. For example:

<u>Computer Skills</u>

Expert in:

    Metastock Professional

    Adobe Photoshop Elements 6

    Microsoft Word

This will capture the reader's interest and get him or her to read your résumé.

The last paragraph is a call to action. Here is an example.

"I am looking forward to hearing from you. I should also say that I will be working on a computer project in the Dominican Republic from January 15 to February 15. I can be reached on my cell phone at 705 321 3190 or by e-mail at <u>johng@rogers.com</u>."

You have done three things: First, you asked the employer to call you; second, you told him or her when you are available and put in a time limit; and finally, you told him or her what you are doing.

Here is a sample letter. Notice how he starts, then lists his most important qualifications, including education, and then indicates how and when he can be reached. The reader of the letter will be interested because, among other things, John Smith has already worked in Yellowknife and wants to go back. Also, Mr. Hall can easily talk to his former employers at Smith and Rollins.

December 17, 2007

Mr. George Hall
Computer Director
Echo Computer Services
160 College Street North
Yellowknife, N.W.T.

Dear Mr. Hall:

I am responding to your advertisement for a computer project manager listed on www.jobsearch.com. I began my search after talking to John Ingram on your management staff.

My supervisory experience along with my computer skills makes me an ideal candidate for this position.

> Bayview Petroleum
> Manager Computer Support. I was responsible for the management of the computer support department for the entire company including the United States operations.

> Master of Science in Computer Science from the University of Waterloo, Waterloo, Ontario.

> During my co-op work term, I worked in Yellowknife for Smith and Rollins doing computer work.

I look forward to hearing from you. I can be reached on my Blackberry at 709 745 8327 or by e-mail at johns@howdy.com. I will be in Buffalo, NY, from January 14 to 16.

Yours truly,

John Smith

Effective Résumés

One of the most important tools is your résumé; I have referred to that before so let's make one. Many résumés are read on a computer, so I show you how to make a traditional résumé and then one for a computer. After that, I tell you how to prepare for a job interview and how to conduct yourself at the interview.

Your cover letter was successful and the hiring manager reads your résumé. Your résumé is the next stage, and it is important that you do this well.

In some cases, you will be required to submit your résumé using e-mail or the company Web site, so you should be ready for that.

The only purpose of a résumé is to get an interview. Look on it as an advertising piece about you. You want to create interest in yourself. You present yourself as someone who can help achieve the goals of the company, department, or organization. It should be tailored to the job you are seeking.

Make sure the spelling and grammar are correct. It should be brief and yet complete, as well as easy to read. Use action verbs and add adjectives if appropriate, such as "successfully trained."

Be truthful; many companies will verify the information in your résumé.

You need to make a lot of copies and give them to everyone who can help you: friends, relatives, or people you meet. Always have copies with you.

The top of the résumé has your personal information including your name, address, e-mail (if you don't have one, get one; this is absolutely essential), home telephone number, Blackberry number, and/or cell phone. Make it easy for people to contact you.

Personal Section

George Somebody	Home telephone	705 728-1234
63 Pine Grove Avenue	Cell	705 325-3456
Barrie, ON	Blackberry/e-mail	somebody@howdy.com
L4N 5Y9		

Job Objective

The second section is your clearly stated job objective. For example:

Food Service Manager

Summary of Qualifications

Below your job objective, put a brief summary of your qualifications. You want to get the attention of the person doing the hiring. For example:

> Experienced manager and cook with six years experience in:
> Volume food preparation
> Food service computer programs
> Kitchen management

Experience

You change the order depending on your age and the job requirements. For example, if you are a recent graduate, then put education first. If you have experience related to the position, put that first.

The section about experience lists your last job first and then you work backward. Include a heading. For example:

<u>Experience</u>

St. Mary's Hospital
May 2004 to present
Chef in charge of kitchen
Produced 1000 meals a day; many of which had to meet special diets

Note that in each case, I included the date, company, and a brief job description. Notice that I used action verbs to describe what was done. Continue on with each position.

Accomplishments

These are things the applicant has accomplished and is able to do. It is brief and to the point. Note that you use an underlined heading. For example:

<u>Accomplishments</u>
Quickly made error-free cash
Trained staff

Managed staff
Reorganized food production
Developed special diet section

Qualifications

Once again, this is brief and lists the abilities the applicant has that relate to the job advertisement. Use an underlined heading.

Qualifications
McDonald's Fast Food Certificate
Ontario Certificate of Qualifications as cook
BS Food and Restaurant Management

Education

List here the relevant education and training you have. For example, give the name of the college and the dates attended. In addition, list seminars that you have taken and that are relevant to the job.

If you are a recent graduate, put this section first.

Education
Time management seminar, May 2007
Management program at Ryerson University, September 2007 to May 2008
BA Food and Restaurant Management, University of Guelph, September 1996 to May 2000
Cook apprentice program at Mount Royal Hospital, Montreal, PQ. May 2001
McDonald's Fast Food Certificate program, May 2000

Community Service
The next section about community activities and hobbies is optional. Some people do not include this section. My advice is include it if it is related to the job. While preparing this section, I looked at a variety of jobs posted on the Internet. In several cases, the job description included the ability to relate to the community. I say this because I

included it for a position I applied for, and it was one of the reasons I was called in for the interview and hired for the job.

References
Include two or three names. Many employers will not check because they assume they will only say positive things.

Here is a sample résumé using this information.

George McLaren   Home telephone 705 728 1234
63 Pine Grove Avenue   Blackberry/e-mail george63@howdy.ca
Barrie, ON
L5R 5Y9
....
Food Service Manager/Cook

Experienced manager and cook with 6 years experience in:
    Volume food preparation
    Food service computer programs
    Kitchen management
Proved successful in volume food preparation with strict cost controls and at the same time received many compliments from patients, staff, and customers.
....
Experience
St. Mary's Hospital, May 2004 to present
Chef in charge of kitchen
Produced 1000 meals a day, many of which had to meet special diets
Supervised 40 kitchen staff

Georgian University, May 2000 to May 2004
Sous Chef for faculty/student dining room kitchen
Produced 500 meals a day
Organized food production
Prepared food for faculty and administrative committee meetings

McDonald's Restaurants, September 1998 to May 2000
Part-time position starting with counter work and then food preparation

Accomplishments	Qualifications
Quickly made error-free cash	McDonald's Fast Food Certificate
Trained staff	Ontario Cook Apprentice Certificate
Managed staff	BS Food and Restaurant Management
Reorganized food production	

Education
Management program at Ryerson University, September 2007 to May 2008
BS Food and Restaurant Management, University of Guelph, September 1996 to May 2000
Completed cook apprenticeship at Mount Royal Hospital, Someplace, ON, May 2000 with top marks. Worked with one of the best hospital chefs in Ontario.

References

Mr. John Smith	Dr. Wilber Jones, Dean
Food Service Manager	Faculty of Business
Mount Royal Hospital	University of Guelph
4000 Second Street	603 Georgian Drive
Someplace, ON	Guelph, ON
519 745 6789	613 678 9345

Scannable Résumés

This information is based on information from www.quintcareers.com and www.the-arnold-group.com.

Scannable résumés have the same content, but the format may be different. The résumé is scanned into the company's database; and the computer will read for relevant experience, education, and position sought.

It will have the same information and order as a traditional résumé, such as position sought, experience, accomplishments, qualifications, and education.

Use the same words and terms as used in the job description. Find a copy and use the same language. The computer will be looking for this. Each company uses different language to describe skills they are looking for.

The format:

- Use standard-sized paper such as 8.5 by 11 inches
- Use standard typeface and normal-size font such as 12 point
- No graphics or shading
- Use capitals for headings, but do not use bold, italics, underlining, bullets, or lines
- If more than one page, put your name at the top of each page
- Print with a high-quality printer such an ink jet or laser printer
- Use white paper
- Send originals, not copies
- Mail flat

If you want to see the difference between a traditional résumé and a scannable one, go to www.quintcareers.com/scannable_resumes.hmtl and click on "Traditional Résumés" and then look at the same one in a scannable format.

SUCCESSFUL JOB INTERVIEW SKILLS

The next step is the job interview. Your cover letter has been read, your résumé looks excellent, and the company calls you in for an interview. You have traveled a long way; now you have eighteen inches to go. The interview is the major step where you bring together your self-assessment, research, and planning.

The major thing to remember is to go for the job as if this is the job you really want. You can always say "no" afterward, but if you blow it, you can't go back and ask for a rerun. Forget any misgivings you may have. Consider this job along with other job offers.

As I said above, interviews have been described as the last eighteen inches. You have done your research, you are fully qualified for the job, it fits your skills, and it is part of your career plan. The last hurdle is the interview. Make sure you cross over it.

Be ready for different formats. Some interviews are one-on-one, and some are with groups. In some cases, the interviewer will do all the talking and one person will be there taking notes. Some interviews have different formats. I heard of a person who interviewed people with his back to them all the time they were being interviewed. Word got around, so people were not surprised and were prepared.

I was interviewed once while having coffee with a group. No one asked me any questions. When the coffee was gone, the interview was over. I felt quite strange afterward. Some time later, one of the people said they would have hired me if I had had a certain qualification, which I did not know about. I guess I should have done more research. Actually, I had the qualification, but no one asked for it.

Some organizations have more than one interview; the first is with someone in the personnel department. The second interview could be in the department where you hope to work. This could be with the manager or with a group; it could also be a walk around the department.

Here are some important points.

First of all, wear appropriate clothing. Wear clean, well-pressed clothing you would wear to work at this place or the clothing your interviewer would wear. If you wear a suit, men, make sure your socks match your suit (no white socks, please), with shoes, shirt, and tie to match. If you are not used to wearing a suit, ask the person who sold you the suit to help you pick out suitable socks, shirt, and tie.

I know a person who did a lot of interviewing. She told me she could always tell a university student who was coming for his first interview. He looked uncomfortable in a suit, and he wore white socks.

Once I was coaching a young man who had just graduated from university. Sure enough, he had on white socks; in fact, they were the only socks he had. We quickly remedied that.

It helps, especially if you are a bit older, to have either a cell phone and/or Blackberry; this shows that you are in touch with modern technology. Make sure they are turned off during the interview but visible. Many young people assume that older people are out of touch technologically.

Get there a few minutes ahead of time.

Men should get a haircut a few days before the interview; if the cut is too new, it might look too stiff. Fingernails should be cut and clean. Make sure you have clean teeth; there's nothing worse than bad breath. Shoes should also be clean. I read somewhere that shoes tell you all about a person.

Women, according to a very successful business friend of mine, need to be well groomed, which includes getting your hair done the day of the interview, dressing appropriately for the interview, and avoiding heavy perfume and unusual hairstyles.

Give a friendly greeting. Look the person in the eye as you introduce yourself. Have a firm, but not too firm, handshake. If it is too loose, you come across as a wimp; if it is too tight, you can actually hurt the person.

Establish rapport with interviewer using the usual pleasantries, like "Nice to meet you," "Nice office," "Read about this great company," "Glad the Yankees won last night," etc.

Be ready to talk about yourself and expand on details in your résumé. Be brief and to the point. This would include your experience, accomplishments, qualifications, skills, and education. Be honest but don't brag. Do not say anything negative about your previous employer.

Display knowledge of the new position and company. I know interviewers who are amazed that someone would come for an interview who does not know anything about the company. Just look it up on Google or Yahoo. If it is not there, find out. It is absolutely fundamental that you know about the company.

Ask about the requirements of the position. Very often, you can find a job description especially if you found the job on the Internet. You can then stress the ways you can meet or exceed the requirements.

Decide in advance what you can do to help the company or organization. This could include: lowering costs, improving production, providing good customer service, and so on. It depends on the organization. For example, a university would be interested in your teaching and research ability or a hospital in patient care. Both are interested in cost control without lowering standards.

It is important that you rehearse your interview. Get a friend to act as the interviewer and have a mock office set up with appropriate props. Get the person to ask you all the usual questions. Here is a list of typical questions. Be brief and to the point.

- Given your skills and abilities, how do you think you can help this company?
- What did you do on your last job? What were your responsibilities?
- What did you like best?
- What did you like least?
- Why did you leave or want to leave your last job? (Be careful here; do not say negative things about your previous boss or company.)
- If you could have made one suggestion to management, what would it have been?
- What have you done that you are proud of?
- Describe the best/worst boss you ever had?
- Would you tell me about the ups and downs of your health in recent years?
- What do you consider your greatest strength?
- What kinds of things bother you most?
- On your résumé, you said ... Please tell us more about that?
- What are your weaknesses?
- Is there anything else I should know about you?

- What questions do you have about the position or company? (Always have some questions to ask.)
- Sometimes you will be asked, "Tell me about yourself." I have had that asked and so I very briefly told them about myself.
- At some stage, the question of salary and benefits will need to be discussed. Try to get as much as possible without being greedy. In some cases, it is a set amount based on years of experience, education, and so on. In other cases, it can be negotiated. The main thing is to make sure you have this settled.

Follow up the interview with a letter. Here is a sample. Make sure you spell the recipient's name correctly and have it typed.

46 Peacock Lane
King City, ON
L4N4D6

September 6, 2007

Mrs. Dianna George, Vice President of Marketing
International Telephone Corporation
56 King Street West
Cambelford, ON
L5N 6M2

Dear Mrs. George:

Thank you for the interview we had last week about possible employment as manager of sales in Cairo, Egypt.

The thought of using my skills and knowledge in that part of the world is very exciting.

I am confident that under your direction, I could make a significant contribution to your company and help establish your company in the Middle East.

I look forward to hearing from you.

Yours truly,

George Smith

HANDLING REJECTION

After the interview, one of three things will happen: You are hired, you are asked to come in for another interview, or you are rejected. I will talk a great deal about how to handle a new job in the next section. Let me say a few words about being rejected.

First of all, don't take it personally. Don't waste emotional energy. Ask yourself why you were rejected. Decide if it was something you can remedy, and then make the appropriate changes.

Sometimes, it was a good thing and the job was not for you. If the manager did not like you, then you are better off working for someone who does. There is nothing much worse than working for a bad boss.

What can you do if you still want the job? Write back a few days later and thank them for considering you and say you are still interested in working for them. About two months later, write or phone again; keep in touch. It may be that the person they hired was a real turkey and the job becomes open again.

Here are the concepts you've learned in this chapter:

- You've developed long-term goals and a comprehensive career plan.
- You've created a short-term action plan that gets you started toward your goals.
- Your personal needs assessment will help you make good choices about your career.
- There are four different ways to apply for a job.
- A professional cover letter and an effective résumé will help you stand out among job candidates.
- You've reviewed successful job interview skills to make an impact on people face-to-face.
- And you've learned to handle rejection.

Great, you are hired. Now what? In the next chapter, I tell you about essential things to do the first week on the job, how to hold on to your job, and how to develop a complete career control plan. The last chapter discusses changing jobs.

CHAPTER FIVE

How to Keep Your Job and Keep Making a Contribution

Well, you have job, what do you do now? In this chapter, I give you a lot of ideas. Read them all and then pick two, three, or more that would be most helpful for you. Pick the ones that will make a difference, the critical ones. Set goals and work on them. Much of the information in these two sections is from *Job & Career Building* by Richard and Peter Arnold. In this chapter, I talk about:

1. What to do the first week
2. The secrets of holding on to a job
3. A dozen vital on-the-job skills
4. Working on an improvement project
5. Developing a personal career control plan

SIX ESSENTIAL THINGS TO DO THE FIRST WEEK ON THE JOB

The first week on the job is crucial to your success, and there are several things you must do. Keep in mind that you are on trial, and it is important that you project the right image from day one.

1. Prepare the Weekend before You Start

First, prepare for the first week during the weekend before you start. Get your clothes ready; be sure to pick something that is suitable for the first day. Then make sure you know how long it takes to get to work; in many parts of North America, the winter driving can be treacherous, so plan ahead. Also spend some time going over the material you have collected and do some thinking about your new job. Try to set some goals, things you need to accomplish the first week, and try to understand your role in your new job.

2. Learn about Your Job

Second, learning about your new job and how to do it is your first priority. You should meet on Monday with your supervisor; if it is not scheduled, then ask to see him or her. At that meeting, your responsibilities will be outlined; be sure to write everything down and feel free to ask questions if there are things you do not understand. Make sure you know what is expected of you. Your supervisor will also help to get you oriented and may introduce you to the key players. Be sure to get everyone's name.

In some companies, they will have an orientation meeting if a number of people are starting at the same time. This will be more general, focused on the company rather than the individual; you will still need to meet with your supervisor to get your personal responsibilities.

You can then start to work and accomplish something.

3. Get to Know the People in Your Area

Third, get to know the people you will be working with—the person on the next desk, next machine, or in the next room. Remember, working is a social game. Keep a little book and get their names in it, but do this in private. People love it when you say their name. After a while, get them to talk about their families and so on. Find out who the wise people are. They are the ones who know how to do the work really well; they know the informal rules. Ask them to help you.

You will also likely be working on a team; this is another group to get to know. You are trying to build up trust. Be positive; avoid the self-made critics.

Get to meet everyone who has a bearing on your job and try to understand what their goals are.

4. Your Workplace

Fourth, find the place where you will be working and get it organized so you can be productive.

If you work in a white-collar position, you need to learn how your computer works, how to access the Internet, how to send and receive e-mails, and so on. If you are in manufacturing, you need to find out where the equipment is, including a computer, and how to work it. In other words, get familiar with your work area.

5. Learn about Administrative Procedures

Every company has administrative procedures for how they operate. The first week, you will probably spend time filling out forms for the personnel office. Use this time to find out about other administrative things like sick time, emergency matters, and visits to the nurse.

You may also be required to complete some reports on a regular basis for groups such as quality control, sales, or as a team member.

You need to learn how to access services such as photocopying, technological support, tool repair, storage of equipment, and obtaining supplies.

6. Learn about Company Organization

Finally, draw your own organizational chart so that you can see who is who. Make a list of the key people. Make sure you recognize the senior people; they often walk around the company. They may have heard that there is a new person in the company, and they may want to check you out.

You must, of course, do all this while learning and doing your own job.

As I said earlier, work to establish friendly relations with people around you.

SECRETS OF HOLDING YOUR JOB

First—and this is hard to remember—you are essentially alone on the job. You have made friends with others and they may like you. But when things go wrong, you are alone. For example, the company decides to downsize or reorganize—fancy words for laying people off. This happens for a variety of reasons. The company is looking for people to lay off. If you are on the list, you are out, and people who are trying to keep their jobs will ignore you. They are trying to protect themselves.

At this point, you may decide that this is not fair, and it probably isn't. You may decide to go on a crusade. My advice to you, unless you are independently wealthy, is do your job and keep your mouth closed and your head down. Maybe they will keep you on longer or not lay you off. However, work on getting a new job or work on your self-employment company because you will likely be laid off in the future. You will find that people will shun you and are no longer your friends.

Second, be a producer. You are hired to do something. Do it to the best of your ability. You were hired because you were the best person; now show your boss that he or she was right. Be warned; some of your fellow employees may not appreciate your success and will try to sabotage your efforts. Keep in mind that you want to please your boss, not your fellow workers.

Third, establish good relations with your supervisor. Here are some ways of developing good relationships:
- Be very competent in your work
- Do all assignments on time, always
- Make a positive contribution at meetings
- Dress appropriately
- Be interested in them as people; find out things you have in common
- Be positive about him or her outside of the office; build her or him up

- Find out what is important to your boss and make it important to you
- Volunteer for projects
- Realize that they are busy people
- Make your boss look good

Here is an example of what I mean; this comes from a friend of mine who was a senior executive. He was never the top person but often reported to the president. He said that the most important thing was what his boss thought was the most important thing. You may not think it is the most important thing, but what you think is not important. That does not mean that you do not discuss things, but it does mean that at the end of the day, the boss is the boss. If you think about it, the alternative is chaos.

Here is a personal example. As I mentioned before, I helped start a community college. My responsibility was starting the continuing education division. We had great success and were able to start a large number of both regular college and special-interest courses. In the spring of the year, the president, my boss, said that I should not put on any more courses that year, and I should instead consolidate the work. He did not want me to bite off more than I could chew, or words to that effect. I am not very good at filing, making out records, and that sort of thing. When we started, the staff consisted of me and a very competent secretary, and things were getting a bit messy, so I did what he wanted me to do.

Here is one more example. Helen Morrison, a woman I knew, always told her new boss that she would do everything she could to make her or him look good. You see, there are lots of people who try to make the boss look bad. Some people spend most of their time complaining about the boss. Avoid these people like the plague.

Fourth, keep a journal of your achievements. This will come in handy at evaluation time. You may think your boss knows all the wonderful things you have done, but the truth is he or she doesn't. He or she is too busy doing his or her job and trying to please his or her boss.

Also keep complimentary e-mails or letters that may come to you. They are helpful at evaluation time and also if you are laid off. You can use them for your next job interview or for legal action if wrongfully dismissed. I first heard about this from a friend who was a college president. He told me that you never know when you might need them.

Fifth, keep looking to the future and follow your career plan. At the end of this chapter, I will give you all the details that should be in your plan. That will include planned training. Also see if you can increase your responsibilities but not at the expense of someone else. Keep your eye on new position postings. You are looking for positions in your area of expertise.

Sixth, volunteer for projects. Sometimes there are projects that would be good for the company but for one reason or another are not done or that someone tried to do but was unable to do. This can help make you a star.

For example, George worked in a college where they wanted to start a printing management program. He had always been interested in printing; I guess it was because his grandfather was a printer. It had always fascinated him, although he was not a printer. So he took on the development of the program. The first thing he did was talk to people in the industry. The first phone call he made was to the owner of one of the largest printing companies in the city where he lived. The owner was absolutely delighted and wanted to start immediately. George got the approval of the college administration to develop the printing management program. He developed an advisory committee, worked with them, researched other similar programs to develop the curriculum, and got the government approvals to offer the program. The college then hired the staff, purchased the equipment, promoted the program, and enrolled the students. This process took about a year to complete.

A Dozen Vital On-the-Job Skills

Here are a dozen vital on-the-job skills.
- Learn to handle your emotions. Try not to let people get under your skin. Some people make a point of doing that; others will have mannerisms that bug you. You probably do things unwittingly that bug other people. You just have to learn how to get along with people. C. S. Lewis said that

one of the main virtues is forbearance. That is putting up with other people's faults and mannerisms.

- Begin each day by being positive. Today is all you have, so make the best of it.
- Treat others the way you want to be treated. This is known as the Golden Rule.
- Know the company goals and your supervisor's goals. Ask about them. You will be surprised at the reaction. Tell your boss you want this information because you can help him or her be more productive. If you work for a large corporation, look the company up on Google or Yahoo Business to get the general goals of the company. There are lots of sources. Your boss has probably given you this information. However, I must warn you, some bosses are not very good and some have only one real goal, and that is survival.
- Ask for the advice of successful people in the company. They may have been there for a long time and have lessening responsibilities, but they know a lot. They are what used to be called "the wise old men or women of the village." Pay special attention to the women; they often have a different and more astute perspective.
- Avoid emotional reactions. People say nasty things or TGW (things go wrong) happens. Take time to consider your response, if any. Sometimes, it is best to let things go and not respond.
- Present solutions to problems, not just problems. Your boss has enough to think about, let alone problems you bring to him or her. Talk about the problem and suggest solutions. It is important to let your boss know if things are not going right, but always accompany the problem with a solution.
- Keep track of your accomplishments and give lots of recognition to others. Be sincere about this. People can smell a phony or someone who is trying to ingratiate himself or herself.
- Do assignments well and on time, always and no excuses. Make sure your boss knows what you are doing and when

an assignment is finished. At one point in my career, I was assistant to the president of the college where I worked. He gave me a variety of assignments to do—some large, some small. Each week, I made a list of the different projects showing completed ones and ones in progress. In that way, we both knew what was happening.

- Keep growing and learning. Take courses, become an expert at what you are doing. In addition, learn things that are not related to your work. I heard of a man who would take an area of study about which he knew nothing and spend three years learning about it. It has been said that if you read three books about a subject, you probably know more than many people—even ones in that field.

- Keep developing your network within the whole company. Get to know your fellow workers and expand your contacts as far as you can in the company. Keep a little notebook and record any pertinent information. Try to remember everyone's name. People like to be called by name. I know a person who did this, and after a while, she could call everyone in the organization by his or her first name.

- Work on improvement projects. This is so important that I will devote a whole section to it.

WORK ON IMPROVEMENT PROJECTS

How do you go about developing improvement projects?

First, make a list of your job duties or functions. Look at your job description to get the details.

Second, think about how you could improve your performance. Do this self-evaluation at the end of every quarter. That is at the end of March, June, September, and December.

Rank the improvement items in order of importance from easy to difficult.

Make the necessary changes. However, before making changes, decide if you need to get the approval of your supervisor.

Sometimes it is difficult to look at your job and evaluate it. Here are three ways to look at your job which you may find helpful. Look at your ongoing responsibilities, then problems to be solved, and finally innovations. You do not need to write down everything, just things that will make a difference.

Ongoing Responsibilities

First, there are ongoing responsibilities which must be seen to. Ask yourself if they can be done more efficiently. Write these ideas down, rank them in terms of priority, and start working on them.

Problems to Be Solved

Second, there are problems that need to be solved. List these and decide if there are ongoing problems. If so, decide how to remedy the situation. Others are occasional ones. However, they need to be solved. So make a list of them and prioritize.

Innovations

The third way to look at your job is in terms of innovations. How can you do things differently? Are there projects you should undertake that are related but are not being done? You might have gone to a seminar or taken a course and you have this great idea. If the change is a major one, you should talk to your supervisor about it, especially if it involves other people.

Now, making innovations is a difficult thing, so you may have to learn how to do this. For example, I remember a man who worked in quality control. He had taken a course in statistical process control. He started measuring the quantity of glue used in the process. He chose glue because it was the most expensive product used in the process. He discovered that the amount of glue used in the process varied greatly. He calculated that if they could control the glue used, the company could save a significant amount of money. He presented it to his boss, and he was told to forget it. I often wonder why it was not accepted.

Once you have an idea for improvement, talk to your supervisor and present the idea in general; get approval to go ahead. You might find your supervisor approves it or has a way of doing it differently. Once this initial step has been taken, go ahead and work on it.

At some stage, you will be asked to make a cost-benefit analysis. How do you make a cost-benefit analysis? First, you find out how much the change would cost the company. The second step is to determine how much it would either reduce costs or increase revenue. Your company probably has some rules about the percentage your project would either increase sales or reduce costs.

For example, let's say your idea would cost the company $20,000. However, it would reduce costs by $25,000. The difference is $5,000 or 25 percent. This would get your manager's attention.

Here are two innovations I recently witnessed.

Firstly, let me tell you about an innovation at the gym where my wife and I try to go at least twice a week. When we first started, they gave us a list of the machines we should work out on. They did not seem to be in any particular order, so we walked around to find the different machines. The other day, we went to the gym and they had rearranged the machines. They were all in a row and numbered. We started at number one and progressed to the end of the row. This was a simple innovation; the only cost would be hiring people to move and set up the machines, but it made it a lot simpler for people like us.

The second innovation was with my online bank statement. I often wondered what the balance was on a daily basis. So I had to get my calculator and figure it out. Now the bank has a put an end-of-the-day balance on my statement so I know my balance on a daily basis. This would mean changing the main computer program.

Here is a major innovation I heard about. A manufacturing plant needed to enlarge their plant, so they built an extension on the side, which effectively doubled the size. It had a passageway at one end of the partition. The machines were quite difficult to move, so they left them in place.

However, the process involved moving material from one machine to another, and some machines were in the old section and others in the new section. They had to move the product from one section to the other. This meant that they had to move the partially finished product down to the end of the plant and back to the machine on the other side of the wall. This not only took time, but also, some of the product was damaged in the process.

In order to decide about taking out the wall completely, they had to decide if it was worth it or not. The decision was made on the basis of a cost-benefit analysis. Before making any changes, they had to decide whether it would reduce costs or increase revenue by a certain percentage. The people in charge of the project had to determine how much it would cost to either remove the wall or move the machines. Then they had to determine how much this change would lower costs and save the company money and thus increase profits.

Don't let this discourage you. Keep on thinking, and be ready. It may be that in a staff meeting, the chair may ask for improvement ideas; this is your chance. Someone said that luck is where preparation meets opportunity.

Make a list of these improvement projects, put them in priority, talk to your supervisor and get his or her approval, and start to work on them.

Here is an example for a person working in quality control. I will only include a few details.

Ongoing responsibilities
- Testing of materials
- Testing finished product
- Analyzing data from the plant

Problems
- Getting accurate data
- Getting changes in procedures to improve quality

Innovations
- Simplify data recording system
- Learn how to implement changes

Continuous Improvement

Another way to look at your job is called "continuous improvement." I don't know who coined the expression, but it is a marvelous way to look at your work. A man by the name of Dr. Edwards Deming went to Japan after World War II to see what he could do to help rebuild the industry there. He also had a profound effect on North American industry. His book is called *Out of the Crisis*. He developed a very simple system, which he called the Deming's Wheel.

Let me explain what that is.

Let's say you want to build a model airplane. You want to design and build it yourself. So you research model airplanes, draw your plans, and make the plane. The big day arrives and you take it on a test flight. It flies okay but has some problems.

So you make some changes, and it flies a little better. You see some more ways to improve its performance, and you make more improvements. Your plane is getting better and better.

Let's analyze what you did. First, you researched model planes and drew a design on paper. Second, you built the plane. Third, you tested the plane by flying it. Fourth, you saw ways to improve it and made the changes. This process of trying and improving can go for a long time, maybe forever, because nothing is perfect.

This is what Dr. Deming taught the Japanese. I was in a seminar where this whole concept was being taught, and the speaker told us about the first Toyota to come to the United States. It was not for sale but was on a test run. It kept breaking down, and they kept fixing it. Gradually, it started to work better. The rest is now history, and Toyota is one of the leading car manufacturers in the world.

So what I am saying is this: Take your own job or area of responsibility and apply the continuous improvement principle. You can also apply it to your life, marriage, hobby, or whatever you are doing. Keep trying to do better.

KEEP GROWING AND LEARNING

The tenth suggestion above was about growing and learning. I would like to expand on that. At the beginning of the book, I talked about two kinds of skills, transferable skills and special knowledge, which are unique to your line of work.

You need to keep trying to improve these areas. For example, if your work includes making public presentations to groups of people, you could consider joining the Toastmasters Club. I know a person who did this, and her speaking ability was greatly improved. She was good before; now she is excellent.

Many organizations will have training seminars you can attend, or they will encourage you take them outside and will cover the costs. I should also note that your personnel records will have a place for training. In most organizations, attending training seminars is looked on very favorably. This kind of training generally will help with your transferable skills.

Most major newspapers have sections on careers. For example, the *Washington Post* and the *New York Times* in the United States and the *Globe and Mail* in Canada have regular articles dealing with different aspects of careers. Major local papers also have regular articles. These newspaper articles are excellent ways to keep up-to-date about employment and career trends. Look up their Web sites for current articles.

The other kind of training has to do with your special knowledge. Competency is essential. If you are a member of a professional organization or you have a designated trade, you will be expected to take a certain number of courses each year to keep your membership or your professional designation. The other reason is that you need to keep up-to-date and do a good job.

You can attend classes or take a course online. These can be regular secondary, college, or university courses or programs or special interest courses.

It is now possible to take courses online. Look up your interest on Google. In a previous section, I referred to training programs you can take from different colleges, universities, and training companies. This is called distance education; it used to be called correspondence courses. You work on your own time in some cases; other times, you have to fit into a schedule. The old way was to send the responses to the school or university by mail. Now it is done by e-mail.

The instruction is done by webinars. I took one recently, and it was very amazing. I sat at my computer and while the instructor was talking, the illustrations and charts were in front of me. We could also ask questions and talk to the instructor. The sound came over my computer. I have also tried to take these on the telephone, but it was not very satisfactory.

In some cases, you are expected to respond by e-mail to the instructor or other students. In other cases, you need to complete assignments each week. This is probably a good thing for those of us who lack the discipline to complete the work on our own.

Other types of distance learning include purchasing a whole course and completing the assignments as you have time. This requires a lot of discipline to keep going.

You may also be asked to take examinations. If the course is through a college or university, you may have to go there for the examination. This information will be given to you when you inquire.

In Canada, there is the Canadian Virtual University, which is a consortium of thirteen universities offering 250 programs and 2,500 courses. The Web site is www.canadianvirtualU.ca. The first university in Canada to offer distance and online education courses was Athabasca University, www.athabascau.ca.

There are dozens of choices for Americans. Look on Google and put in "online universities." It also lists universities outside North America.

The Open University offers online courses in the United Kingdom. The Web site is www.open.ac.uk.

In addition, your local community college or institute of technology offers continuing education and online courses. Ask Google for "Online courses at …"

I should also add that many courses are on DVDs or cassette tapes which you can purchase at any good bookstore. Many commuters listen to CDs on the way to work. The point I am trying to make is that training is available for people who cannot attend classes.

It seems that every time I turn my computer on, I see an advertisement for a university or college offering undergraduate and graduate degrees. Some are from Canada, some from the United Kingdom, and others are from the United States.

I really believe that growing like this helps you as a person. This is especially true when you retire. Some people vegetate, go crazy, or die an early death. So keep growing and learning.

Develop a Personal Career Control Plan

You can put all the information you have developed into a personal career control plan and keep it in a three-ring binder. This plan will help you control your career. This may seem like a lot of work, but remember, you are working on a million-dollar project, so plan well and work your plan.

The components of your plan are:

1. Your skills inventory
2. Your top-ten special knowledge areas or skills
3. Statement in goal form of two job targets to be achieved in the next three to five years
4. Position evaluation forms
5. Interview records
6. Contact lists
7. Career planning worksheets
8. Development activities and learning projects
9. Different Ways to Move in Your Career
10. Personal needs assessment worksheets
11. Short-term action plan
12. Job enrichment ideas
13. Organization chart
14. Career progress
    a) Yearly goals
    b) Quarterly goals
    c) Summary of accomplishments. Record every achievement or accomplishment that you can legitimately take credit for, such as solving a problem, suggesting a solution, or presenting new ideas.

Include your objectives and how you met them. In some cases, this will be part of your evaluation. In some organizations, your supervisor will work with you on developing your objectives and how you can achieve them. This will be the basis for your next evaluation.

Make a summary each month and group according to objectives. Also include development activities such as reading, seminars, workshops attended, and so on.

NEXT STEPS

You have been doing a lot of thinking and working on your career. How much success you achieve depends on what you do in the next three or four days.

So please complete the following. It is designed to give you a jump start on your career.

The first thing I am going to do to control my career is _____

_____

_____

_____

By when?

_____

_____

_____

_____

Other people who will be involved or affected _____

_____

_____

_____

Consequences of action _____

_____

_____

_____

Consequences of inaction

_____

_____

_____

_____

_____

In this chapter, I have given you advice to help you hold on to your job.

- You've learned the six essential things to do the first week on the job.
- The secrets of holding on to your job have been reviewed.
- You know a dozen vital on-the-job skills.
- You've learned that working on improvement projects can aid your career.
- You'll keep growing and learning.
- You've developed a career control plan.

Once you have decided on a course of action, expect opposition and probably fear. You will find yourself swimming against the current of people's expectations. People are always putting a heavy expectation on others and may not be able to handle a successful, proactive person. There are some people who will discourage you by saying, "You can't do that."

You may also experience fear from within. Am I doing the right thing? What will happen if ...? You need to have inner resources to help you.

It is easy to sit back and let it all happen to you; it is difficult to make it happen—especially if it is just you.

Good things come to an end, and in the next section, I talk about leaving your present job and getting another.

CHAPTER SIX

HOW TO MOVE UP OR MOVE ON

"As long as I am president, you will have a job." Three weeks later, you are given your severance pay and you are unemployed. This may have been caused by a company buyout, a takeover, a plant closure, or other unforeseen circumstances. We read regularly in the papers about companies laying off thousands of employees. It happens. What do you do about it? That's what this section is all about.

This is the difficult part. You decide to leave or the decision is made for you through retirement, layoff, plant closures, or dismissal with or without cause. The result is the same: you are no longer working.

Or you may have been working for several years and start thinking about changing your job within your company or leaving your job and working either as a self-employed person or working for someone else.

FIVE DIFFERENT WAYS TO MOVE IN A COMPANY

This section is for people who are already employed and are wondering what they should do next, if anything. We often think that there is only one way to move and that is up into the next level. In this section, I will show you five ways to move in an organization. I have illustrated this in the following chart. There is also one at the back, which you can photocopy. These ideas are from *Up Is Not the Only Way* by Dr. Beverly Kaye. This excellent book gives a complete analysis of career management within an organization.

The first option is to simply expand your present job into what you want. Use the chart below. Fill in the part in the middle that shows where you are at present. Put in the name of your position.

Donald Ford

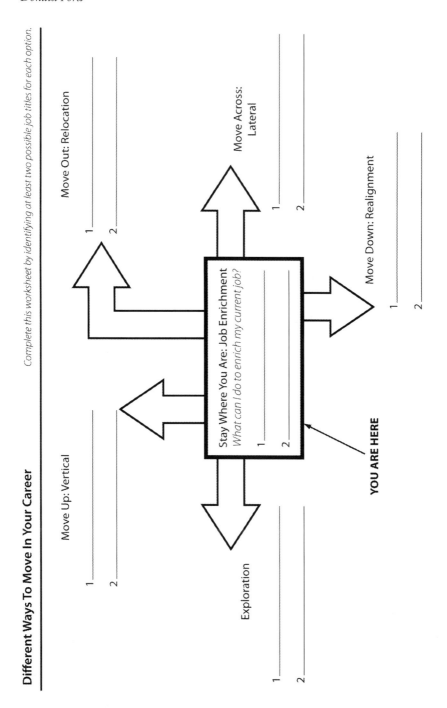

Different Ways to Move in Your Career

104

Then ask yourself, "What can I do to enrich my present position?" Write down two or three things you could do. It is important to keep growing on your job and improving your ability. This is called continuous improvement. I talked about that in the last chapter.

If you want to move, start looking at the different options. Put these options on the chart. You need to be discrete about these investigations. This is not an actual move but simply an investigation. You want to find out if these fit your skill set. You can find this out by talking to the person who currently holds the job or looking up the job description in the personnel office. You need to decide if your skills fit the job; if not, get the additional training. When an opening occurs, you can apply for it and will probably get it because you have done your research.

For example, George Lewman wanted to learn the business in quite a large company. He started in accounts payable and after a while got a job in accounts receivable, working without extra pay. In this way, he learned about other jobs. His goal was to learn the business. This is an unusual example, but it is one way to find out what is needed.

As I have said before, you need to realize that there will not be a perfect fit, so you need to find out the areas in which you may have difficulty—the occupational shoals, land mines, and icebergs that can wreck a career. These are your weaknesses. These small things can wreck your career. Decide if you can handle these areas, and if not, figure out what you are going to do about it.

Here are two examples of what I mean by looking at the whole job.

In a previous example, I talked about Duncan, the nurse. Nurses, in addition to regular nursing care, also have to be able to handle unruly patients. I was surprised to learn from talking to nurses in large hospitals that nurse physical abuse by upset patients can be a real problem. Duncan decided to do something about an abusive patient and restrained his arms so that he could not punch the other nurses. He got in trouble with the hospital; he should have talked to his supervisor before taking any action and as a result has a negative letter in his file.

Look at the job description. Be very honest with yourself, and rate yourself on the different aspects of the job. Often, a job description will include duties with challenges such as handling difficult customers or staff.

Here is another example. I looked at the job description for a financial services representative for a large bank. The main job is identifying customer needs for various banking services; however, it also requires that the employee keep accurate records. The main part of the job is sales; the area of potential weakness is accurate record keeping.

For example, let's say you are very good at sales and always exceed your quota. However, you also need to keep your credibility and you might be tempted to stretch the truth or even tell a lie. After a while, people find out and you are finished; no one will buy from you. Quite regularly, we read about someone in a public position who commits some type of misdemeanor. The papers get ahold of it, and the person is finished.

These weaknesses do not have to be dishonest actions; they could be things such as not being able to work in a group when your job requires you to do so.

The second option is moving up in the company. Once again, research the position by talking to people and looking up the job description in the personnel office. Be discrete about this because people could think that you are trying to get their job. Once again, if you want to move, you will very likely need to upgrade your qualifications; you will find the needed qualifications in the job description.

For example, you are a member of a team that deals with very technical matters, and you are very good at what you do. If you want to be team leader, which is the next step up, you will need to learn how to lead and act as a team leader. The same bank referred to above has details of the team leader's job which are quite different from those of a member of the team and include responsibilities such as: overseeing the team, coaching, providing annual reviews, maintaining or exceeding targets, and so on.

The third option is a lateral move. This is related to the first option, that is, researching a position. Moves like this can help you learn more about the business and are often a way to get promoted. It will also add variety to your work. It may even be a better fit with your skills and abilities.

For example, Dan Small was appointed manager of an organization that recruited men and women to work overseas, sometimes under difficult circumstances. Prior to this appointment, he had lived in one of the countries where they sent people and knew what was involved. He did a reasonable job but was not comfortable with handling his staff. He did not have the internal strength needed to make hard decisions, nor did he know the laws governing employment. His strength was in his ability to create a vision. He lacked the skills needed to implement his vision; he was not able to get his staff onside with him. At the same time, he was working on an advanced degree related to his work.

He has had a lateral transfer and now has an important position with the same organization; he is an internal consultant, a position which fits his skills much better. He works with different groups giving advice on how they can do a better job.

The fourth option is realignment or moving down. Sometimes people work hard and get promoted to a management position. This involves a lot of new skills and responsibility, which is often taken home. I know of people who decide that they have enough pressure at home with family without the added pressure of work, so they move down into their former position.

Sometimes, as more senior employees get older, they are asked to take a demotion, which can be quite difficult to do. The best thing to do is take it and swallow your pride. This might also be the trigger to do something different.

Frank McAlister, age thirty-five, worked in a charitable organization and had considerable administrative skills when working under a senior person. He decided to go on and get a master's degree in administration. After graduation, he was promoted to the position of director of a major division of the same organization. The existing staff had difficulty accepting him, and he was not tough enough to lead them. He had the administrative skills to run the organization but not the internal strength to provide the leadership needed. He found it difficult to take the senior leadership position.

An assistant directorship came open, and he was then appointed as an assistant director in a different division. This fit him exactly, and I heard him say, "I am a number-two person." I watched him organize and run a large international conference for five hundred or more people who came from different countries, so I know he had the administrative skill to do that. However, he does not have the emotional strength to make the hard decisions required of a senior leader, nor is he a visionary. He works best when someone else has the vision; he then can bring the vision into reality. He has found his niche and now is in demand as an assistant director.

The fifth option is moving out and getting a job in a different company or choosing self-employment. If possible, get the new job before leaving your present one. It is easier to get a new job if you are already employed. I talked about getting a new job and self-employment in the last chapter.

DECISION TO LEAVE OR STAY

First of all, if you have the option, don't leave until you have a better place to go. In other words, you want to go into a place rather than leave where you are. The emphasis is on going into a better place rather than leaving.

Second, redo all the research I have outlined under the section, "What are your skills?" You probably have a lot of new skills or are better at what you do. Next, do the research outlined in the section, "Where Do You Want to Work?" before making a change. This may be difficult because you are still working.

Third, realize that as you get older, three things can happen: Either you will keep moving up the ladder and get more responsibilities, your upward movement will stop, or you will be demoted. Don't leave because your upward movement has stalled. It is my advice to swallow your pride and keep doing your job. You can always improve your performance using some of the ideas in the previous section.

The other thing I want to mention is that you may not be recognized for what you have accomplished over the years. In fact, they may treat you badly. Don't be surprised; just be thankful when you are treated with dignity and respect. I find it helpful to realize that we live and work in an imperfect world.

It is also important for your own sake that you keep growing; otherwise, you turn into a vegetable. Keep taking seminars and courses and reading. This could be work related or you could pick something you don't know anything about and learn about it.

Also, as your responsibilities decline, you can start doing volunteer work; most organizations and churches I know about are always looking for more help. The skills and contacts you pick up doing volunteer work can also be applied to your regular work. Be sure to add them to your accomplishment lists. As I said before, one of the reasons I got hired was my work in a volunteer organization.

Finally, if you decide to go the self-employed route, don't leave your job until the income you receive from self-employment replaces your income from your present employment. Be careful here because some organizations will put pressure on you to leave before this happens. They will say you must work full-time or not at all.

When you leave, don't bad-mouth your previous employer. Leave on good terms with everyone. In this world, you need all the friends you can get. Don't do anything to create enemies or make people not like you. It may be that you will want to have your previous employer as a client. Your previous employer will also probably be called by any prospective employer. You want them to say good things about you. Also, a bad-mouthing person does himself or herself a lot of harm emotionally. You need to forgive people who hurt you. Carrying around bad feelings will hurt you but will not hurt the other person.

HOW CAN I TELL IF IT IS TIME TO LEAVE?

This is very difficult, especially since it may involve moving to another city or commuting. As I said before, look at the options and how this will affect you and your family. Sometimes, a lot of pressure is put on you to leave and the best thing to do is to go.

There are several internal signs. First, you may be relieved of your responsibilities by your supervisor and you go to work with nothing to do. Second, you may be moved to a very demeaning office, such as in the basement or a warehouse. Third, they stop inviting you to meetings even though you are part of the group. Finally, you may be falsely accused of some misdemeanor. There may be other indicators that the end is near, so face reality and seriously start looking for a new job.

This is a survival game, so take it very seriously and get to work getting a new job. Here are two examples of the above situation which I have personally observed.

The first story is about the head of a major hotel chain. We were interested in having some of our students working for his hotel chain. I found his office in the basement of one of the largest hotels. It was in kind of an open area; I was not sure what to say, but I know that about six months later, he was looking for a new job.

The second is about a man named Murray. He had an office job, and his new boss decided that Murray had to go. So instead of just laying him off, he took his work away from him, and Murray went to work with nothing to do. Eventually, they did lay him off.

How do you decide what to do? One of the best decision-making tools I know is very simple. Take a piece of paper and divide it in half. At the top of the left half, write down the pros of the change and on the right half the negatives. This will help you make an informed decision.

The other thing to do is talk to a wise friend or your mentor. Tell him or her the whole story: your situation at work, what you are thinking of doing, and how this will affect your life. You must make your own decision, but a trusted wise friend or mentor can see things you cannot see. I remember doing this once when I had this great idea. I can still hear my friend, Les, saying, "Well ..." and then a big, long pause. He pointed out things I never thought about, and I abandoned the idea quickly. I have been thankful ever since.

A while back, I asked Harry Webb, a friend of mine who worked in an occupation where they reported to a volunteer board and had a high turnover, about when to leave a job. In that occupation, very often, there were only a few employees and the rest of the work was done by volunteers. I asked him what the secret of working in that situation was. He said, "Quit before they kick you out." Maybe that is good advice.

DISMISSAL WITH OR WITHOUT CAUSE

Let's look at dismissal with or without cause.

First of all, you are fired, dismissed, or whatever you want to call it because of something you did or did not do.

Your first step is to ask yourself, "What did I do wrong?" Be honest with yourself, and then try to figure out how to change your behavior. You might also want to consider that you are not suited for that job.

The next step is to start the career process from the beginning. That is "What are my skills?" followed by "Where do I want to work?" and then "How can I get there?" In other words, start the job-getting process from the beginning. You have probably learned a lot of new skills, so be sure to incorporate them.

Now a few words about dismissal without cause. You are a good employee, but for some reason, you are laid off. This could be the result of general layoffs, new management who want to bring in their own staff, or somebody decides they don't like you. Who knows why things happen? So the reality is that you don't work there anymore. Often, there are signs that things are not going well. As soon as you notice some of the symptoms, get busy looking around. It may be that when you are laid off, you can get a new job quickly or your self-employment company will take off.

Again, first, ask yourself: "What went wrong? Is there something I did that caused my dismissal?" Be honest with yourself and then decide how you could change your behavior.

Second—and this will sound like a broken record—don't spend emotional energy running down your previous employer. This may be very difficult. Perhaps the best way to handle it is to write it all down or talk to your mentor.

It is sort of like going through the grieving process. Grieving is the result of a significant loss. A job could very well be like that, especially if you liked it, you did it well, and it was significant. All of a sudden, what was very important is not there anymore and there is a big, empty hole in your life. On Monday morning, you stay home; this can be very traumatic. It can also be a big relief especially if you have been treated badly.

Third, do the self-assessment again; you have probably learned a lot of new skills. Then do the research of jobs in your area of interest. You might also consider self-employment if you have a good severance package or are eligible for some type of unemployment insurance. You might also use this as an opportunity to consider changing your field of work. If you want to change, there are training programs to help you do that. I talked about that in the previous section. However, in general, it is best to stay in your field of expertise.

Let me say another word about severance pay. You may have received a good severance package. The temptation is to think you have lots of time to get established again. My advice is don't count on it. It may take longer than you think, and all of a sudden, your pay is about to run out and panic sets in.

If you want to take a brief holiday, do so, but when you return, your full-time job is to get another job. Write out your goals and plan of action. As a friend of mine used to say, "Plan your work, and work your plan." Work at it nine to five until you are established again. If you are working at home, go into your office, shut the door, and explain to your family that you are working at home for awhile. If you cannot work at home, go to the library or someplace where you can work.

Here is an example of what I mean. A few years ago, my wife and I were overnight guests in a home. The husband had just been laid off from a very important job. At breakfast, he explained that he had to leave as soon as possible to work on getting a new job. Right after breakfast, he was gone, looking for work.

I have said this before, but you must have an e-mail service. It is assumed that you have one. If you do not, get one today.

There are a number of career centers run by colleges and government organizations. They may be able to help. Some are helpful; some are not.

The final step is to market yourself. Go through all the steps outlined previously in chapter four.

There are some special situations that you need to be ready for.

The first situation you need to be ready for is explaining why you left your previous employer. During your job interview, you will be asked, "Why were you laid off?" Be straightforward. If you were laid off with cause, tell what happened, what you have learned, and how you plan to remedy the situation.

In some cases, you may have a gap in your employment record. This may be due to various reasons such as going back to school, staying home to look after your family, illness, or other such reasons. First of all, do not put that on your résumé. It will probably show as a gap on your résumé. You will be asked what you were doing between one date and the other. Be straightforward. Tell what happened and how you are remedying the situation.

Second, you may have to start at the bottom again; don't waste everyone's time by applying for a fairly senior position similar to the one you had before. It is like any other new job; you have to prove yourself.

Make the person who hired you glad he or she did. Depending on your circumstances, you may want to avoid any situation that would possibly get you in trouble again.

In this chapter, I have given some advice about the most difficult part of working—namely, changing jobs. The main points covered were:

- Making the decision to leave or stay
- Knowing how to tell if it is time to leave
- Understanding that dismissal, with or without cause, is difficult but can be managed

It is important that you learn how to change jobs with as little stress as possible. In the conclusion, I emphasize the main points and encourage you to take action and control of your career.

CONCLUSION

Well, we have come a long way. Let's review the main steps of your journey toward taking control of your career.

- First, get to know yourself. What do you want to do with your life? What do you really like doing? What are your skills? What do you know? How can you put this together in a saleable package? Also, know your weaknesses; these are the things that can get you into trouble.
- Second, where do you want to work? Do you want to work in your city or are you prepared to commute? If so, how far? How will this change affect your family? Do you want to start your own business?
- Third, how do you get the job you want? Network, apply directly, look on the Internet, or all of these ways? Are you ready for the all-important interview and follow-up?
- Fourth, how do you handle the first week on the job, keep growing, and relate to other employees and especially your supervisor?
- Finally, keep your career control plan up-to-date. Do this every three months, that is, at the end of March, June, September, and December. You never know when you will need it. As I said before, "luck is when preparation meets opportunity."

Let me conclude with a pair of true stories.

√ Case Study: Dorothy

Dorothy is a very outgoing person, and while in high school, she got involved in a club that organized conferences for students during the spring break. She took the English co-op course at university. Before deciding what to do on her first work term, she did skills analysis, much the same as I have outlined. She decided that she liked the conference business and also liked writing.

On two of her work terms, she worked in the conference business, and on her last work term, she worked for a software company writing manuals in a language that people could understand. She spent all day working at her computer. The company was located about five hours from all her friends.

She tried out two different jobs and decided on the conference business. She liked the software company, and they liked her, but she was an outgoing person and liked being close to her friends, so she decided to get into the conference-planning business.

Her first job was with a professional organization. Her boss was an older person without much drive, so Dorothy started looking around. She found a job with a large conference-planning company and did quite well. She was in charge of transportation and special events. Sometimes, she had as many as seventy or more buses to look after. On one occasion, she had to put up a large tent in downtown Toronto which involved getting building permits and so on. The special event was for an internationally known music group.

However, it seemed that everything she did was always criticized in detail. After a while, this started to get to Dorothy, and as she told me, it was to her a poisoned atmosphere.

So once again, she started to look around and talked to a friend who was in the financial-planning business. She had to develop a new knowledge base in investments, insurance, and mutual funds.

She was changing her field of work but still used many of her skills of relating to people, taking initiative, and so on. She passed all the exams the first time she wrote them and started in her new line of work.

Dorothy left the conference company on good terms and was able to sign up several of her former associates as clients.

She is doing quite well but has one area of weakness which seems to be an obstacle in her path. She finds it difficult to recruit others to work for her in order to make her business grow. Her husband has a business background and is joining her as a partner. It will be interesting to see if together they can overcome this obstacle.

It is important that you act on what you have learned and that you develop an action plan. So please complete the following plan.

I plan to do the following three things to get control of my career:

1._____

_____

_____

_____

2._____

_____

_____

_____

3._____

_____

_____

_____

I plan to have them completed by:

1. Date ___/___/_____
2. Date ___/___/_____
3. Date ___/___/_____

I am going to make myself accountable to: _____

_____

_____

_____

√ Case Study: Abigail

Here is another story that will encourage you. Abigail was married to a man who had polio. They had two small children, and as result, they were not able to make ends meet. They lived in a medium-sized city in Western Canada. Abigail was very persistent and courageous and decided that if they were going to survive, she had to go to work; however, with two small children, that meant working at home.

In those days, three jobs were open to women: nursing, teaching, and secretarial work. Nursing and teaching were out of the question, so she chose secretarial work. She did not know how to type, so she bought a typewriter and taught herself how to type. Then she went to the lawyers in her city and asked if they had any typing that needed to be done. They did, and she started her business.

Gradually, she built her business from typing to printing. This grew until she had thirty people working for her. She decided to join the chamber of commerce; they did not have any women members at that time but decided to let her join largely because she had the largest printing plant in their city. She finally retired and sold her business.

As I said at the beginning, many companies are in transition because of a number of factors. These could include a changing economic climate, new senior management, downsizing, plant closures, and so on. These mean unusual challenges for people entering the job market, those already employed, and those who have been laid off.

It is essential that you know how to control your career; no one can do this for you. In this book, I have emphasized the following points:

- Controlling your career is of the utmost importance.
- You have a unique set of skills and knowledge.
- Know what you are good at and what you find satisfying.
- Find a job where you can make a contribution to the success of the company.
- Practice the skills for keeping your job.
- Learn how to change jobs with the least amount of stress.
- Be accountable to someone and seek advice.

- Make and work your career control plan.

I trust that you have found this book helpful and that you will find a very satisfying and productive career that will provide for your needs and the needs of your family and also make the world a better place.

Henry Ford once said, "One of the greatest discoveries a man or woman can make, one of the greatest surprises is to find that they can do what they thought they couldn't do."

APPENDIX

LIST OF CHARTS

Please make photocopies of these charts.

My Accomplishments
My Top Seven Accomplishments
Skills Priority List
Special or Technical Knowledge
My Weaknesses
Different Ways to Move in a Company
People Preferences
Information Interview Record
Summary of Things to Research
Comprehensive Career Control Plan
Six-Month, Short-Term Action Plan
Personal Needs Assessment Plan
Personal Career Control Plan

My Accomplishments

Ages   1–10

11–20

21–30

31–40

41–50

My Top Seven Accomplishments

Be sure to leave a wide margin for space to note your skills.

First Accomplishment	Skills

Second Accomplishment	Skills

Third Accomplishment	Skills

Donald Ford

Fourth Accomplishment	Skills

Fifth Accomplishment	Skills

Sixth Accomplishment	Skills

124

Seventh Accomplishment	Skills

Donald Ford

Skills Priority List

Transferable Skills
1.
2.
3.
4.
5.
6.
7.
8.
9.
10.

Operating Relationships

Relationship Skills

Values

126

Special or Technical Knowledge

Special Knowledge I Picked Up in School or College

Special Knowledge I Picked Up at Work or at Home

Donald Ford

Special Knowledge I Picked Up at Seminars or Workshops

Special Knowledge I Picked Up by Reading or Talking to People

My Weaknesses

My Weaknesses in Relation to People

My Weaknesses in Relation to Ideas or Information

My Weaknesses in Relation to Things

Different Ways to Move in a Company

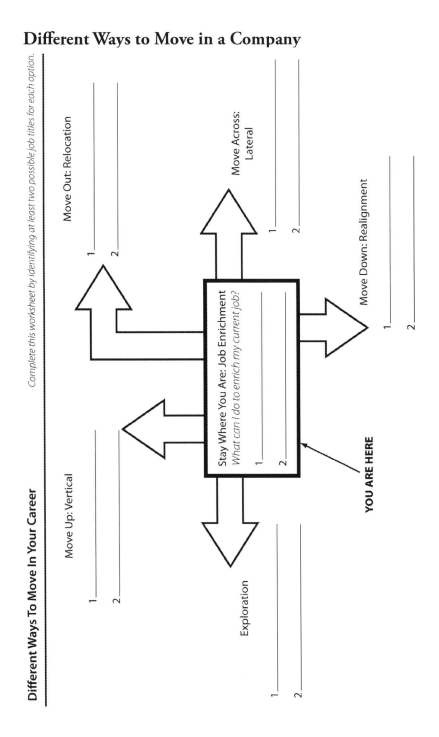

Complete this worksheet by identifying at least two possible job titles for each option.

Different Ways To Move In Your Career

Move Out: Relocation

1 _____

2 _____

Move Across:
Lateral

1 _____

2 _____

Move Up: Vertical

1 _____

2 _____

Stay Where You Are: Job Enrichment
What can I do to enrich my current job?

1 _____

2 _____

YOU ARE HERE

Move Down: Realignment

1 _____

2 _____

Exploration

1 _____

2 _____

People Preferences

Characteristics of People Who Drain Me

Characteristics of People Who Help Me Grow and Develop

Donald Ford

Information Interview Record

Date: _____
Name of person interviewed: _____

Telephone/e-mail: _____
_____

Position: _____
Department: _____

Names of others in the department: _____
_____

What was said: _____
_____
_____
_____
_____
_____

What skills are needed: _____
_____
_____
_____
_____
_____

Date thank-you note was sent. (Make sure you have the correct
spelling of names and that it is typed.) _____
_____

Summary of Things to Research

This will help you think about the different issues involved in researching a job. Some items may not be important or relevant; skip these. Only look at the items that are relevant to the jobs you are interested in.

Skills/strengths/weaknesses

Supervisor

People in department or company

Characteristics of new department or company

Compensation package

Potential for personal growth

Shift work/hours expected

Geography

Comprehensive Career Control Plan

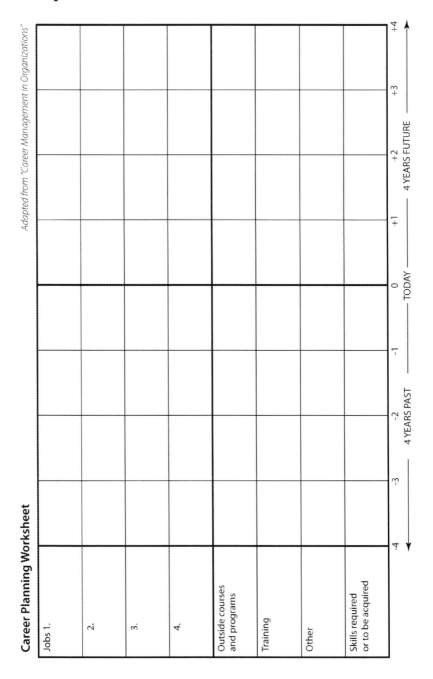

Career Planning Worksheet

Adapted from "Career Management in Organizations"

	-4	-3	-2	-1	0	+1	+2	+3	+4
Jobs 1.									
2.									
3.									
4.									
Outside courses and programs									
Training									
Other									
Skills required or to be acquired									

4 YEARS PAST — TODAY — 4 YEARS FUTURE

Six-Month, Short-Term Action Plan

Name _____

Date _____

Objective _____

_____

Action	Who	By When	Amount of Time	Cost	Date Finished

Personal Needs Assessment Plan

This plan will help you zero in on specific skills needed for your next job. Note that you need to put in two targeted positions and the date you will be ready for a transfer, promotion, outside position, or self-employment.

The first column lists the required skills or special knowledge. Rate yourself, and record the results in the second column. The last column lists the training required.

Name _____ Date _____

Current Position _____

Targeted Position #1 _____ Ready date _____

Targeted Position #2 _____ Ready date _____

Required Skills or Special Knowledge	Rating 1 low 5 high	Required Now X Future O	Development Activity Required	Training Required

Personal Career Control Plan

Use this as a list of things you need to put in your personal career control plan. Get a three-ring binder and keep everything together.

- Transferable skills inventory
- Special skills or technical skills inventory
- Job targets to be achieved in the next two years
- Position evaluation forms
- Information interview records
- Contact lists
- Comprehensive career control plan worksheets
- Development activities and learning projects
- Personal needs assessment worksheets
- Short-term action plan
- Job enrichment ideas
- Different ways to move in a company
- Organization chart
- Career progress
- Yearly goals
- Quarterly goals
- Summary of accomplishments—Record every achievement or accomplishment that you can legitimately take credit for, such as solving a problem, suggesting a solution, or implementing new ideas.

Bibliography

Bowles, Richard Nelson. *The New Quick Job Hunting Map.* Berkeley, California: Ten Speed Press, 2000.

Burack, Elmer H., and Nicholas J. Mathys. *Career Management in Organizations.* Lake Forest, Illinois: Brace-Park Press, 1980.

Deming, Edwards. *Out of the Crisis.* Cambridge, Massachusetts: MIT Press, 1986.

Germann, Richard, and Peter Arnold. *Job and Career Building.* Berkeley, California: Ten Speed Press, 1980.

Kaye, Beverly. *Up Is Not the Only Way.* Mountain View, California: Davies-Black, 2002.

Kranendonk, Dick L. *Serving as a Board Member.* Belleville, Ontario: Essence Publishing, 2000.

Schein, Edgar H. *Career Dynamics.* Reading, Massachusetts: Addison-Wesley Publishing Company, 1978.

Wallach, Ellen J. *The Job Search Companion.* Harvard, Massachusetts: The Harvard Common Press, 1984.

SUGGESTED READING

Bowles, Richard Nelson. *What Color Is Your Parachute?* Berkeley, California: Ten Speed Press, 2009.

Carnegie, Dale. *How to Make Friends and Influence People.* New York, New York: Simon and Schuster, 1990.

Miller, Arthur F., and Ralph T. Mattson. *The Truth about You.* Berkeley, California: Ten Speed Press, 1989.

HELPFUL WEB SITES

www.athabascau.ca
www.bls.gov/home.htm
www.canadabusiness.ca
www.canadianvirtualU.ca
www.careerbuilder.ca
www.cdm.uwaterloo.ca
www.DirectResponseJobs.com
www.jobbank.ca
www.monster.ca
www.occupationalinfo.org
www.onlineoption.com
www.ontariojobfutures.ca
www.open.ac.uk
www.quintcareers.com
www.self-counsel.com
www.servicecanada.ca
www.the-arnold-group.com
www.themompreneur.com
www.usa.gov/Business/Self_Employed
www.weddles.com
www.workopolis.com

If you think this book would be helpful to your friends, copies can be ordered at:

www.chapters.indigo.ca
www.amazon.com
www.iuniverse.com